KINGSTONE
HERO DEVOTIONS

VOLUME 1

Written by **Ben Avery**

Art by **Danny Bulanadi, Mario Ruiz, Sergio Cariello, and Noval Hernawan**

Lettered by **Ben Avery**

KINGSTONE
COMICS

CONTENTS

Published by Kingstone Comics
www.KingstoneMedia.com
Copyright © 2012
Printed in the United States of America

KINGSTONE
COMICS

Introduction:
"You Don't Need a Cape to Be a Hero"

by Ben Avery

When I was a kid, I used to tie a blanket around my neck, put on my winter gloves (even in the summer) and rain boots (even on the driest days), and put on a little mask that only covered my nose and eyes but made it almost impossible to see and then, hot and sweaty and nearly blind, I'd ride my bike around our yard.

Why?

Because that's what I saw when I saw heroes. In my comic books and on TV and on the movie screen, heroes had capes, boots, and masks. That's what they looked like, so that's what I wanted to look like. With my cape I could fly and my bike would become an awesome car with incredible gadgets. (In my grandparents' house, there is still a picture hanging on the wall of little Benjy Avery riding his bike in full superhero gear.)

And I didn't just want to be like those heroes on the outside, I wanted to do the things those heroes did. They rescued people who needed help and stood up to bad guys and helped people escape tornadoes and earthquakes and fires. They had courage to do the right thing, even when it was difficult to do.

Heroes were cool.

But they were also imaginary.

This book is full of REAL heroes. There are bad guys and people who need help and even an earthquake and some fires, yes, but more importantly there are men and women who were heroes.

When you use this book, I hope you see that you can be a hero. When you and I think about superheroes, we can't do what they do. We can't fly or blast lasers out of our eyes. But we can be like these heroes.

When you look at these heroes -- these REAL heroes -- we see what a hero looks like. Not the way little Benjy Avery did, with the gear and the bright colors and the capes and the masks. Instead, you will see what they look like in their lives. Looking at their lives, we see people who lived the way God wants us to live.

The truth is, you can be a hero. And in this book, you will find thirteen stories of heroism. You will find thirteen character traits that a real hero has. You will find thirteen verses you can memorize to help you remember these examples of how to be a hero. You will find thirteen examples that you can learn from to be a hero yourself.

And you don't even need a cape.

~ Ben

How To Use This Book

This book contains thirteen character traits taken from thirteen Bible stories, and it can be used many different ways.

Each character trait is divided into five sections, and each section has a couple of questions to think about or to use as discussion starters plus an "Action Activity."

Part One: a short comic featuring the story. The scripture that the story is found in has also been included, if you want to look deeper into the story.

Part Two: a description of the character trait. These character traits are called "Hero Traits" in this book, and in this section they are defined.

Part Three: a Bible verse about the character trait. These verses go along with the topics, but they were selected because they are powerful reminders of what it means to be a follower of Christ. Some are promises, some are commands, and all are worth knowing (even for adults!) and having in our mind, ready to use when we face difficult situations. Memory cards are included in the back of the book (you can cut them out or copy them) to help you learn these important verses. (The author still remembers some verses he learned when he was a kid, even now, thirty years later, when he faces situations as an adult!)

Part Four: what the character trait looked like in the story. This section explores how the people in the story had this "Hero Trait."

Part Five: what the character trait looks like in our lives. This section explores what the "Hero Trait" is like for us in the here and now, not just reading or hearing stories, but living it out ourselves.

Finally, the "Action Activity" is a simple activity that gives a hands-on example of the "Hero Trait."

So, how can this book be used? It has been designed to be used in multiple ways, depending on settings and circumstances.

1. As a Family Bible Study. Each of the five sections are short enough to be used as a family devotional time each weekday (perhaps before bedtime or after dinner). The first day, read the story, and the days following, read the other parts and use the questions to start some discussions about the topics. The verses found in part three of each devotion could be memorized as a family, possibly by making a game out of it. (Don't forget to pray together after you've spent time talking about the story and the trait!) And if your family cannot find time to do something daily, the devotions are not very long even if you went through all five parts in one sitting, maybe on that one evening when you can sit together as a family. And the "Action Activity" works as a fun family activity that could lead to conversations about the topic. In our busy, fast paced lives, having time set aside to talk and pray as a family is important, and this book is designed to help do that.

2. As a Personal Bible Study. The devotions found in this book can also be used alone in the same way. A child who does daily devotions could use this book. A child who just likes to sit down and read could use it as well. Again, the design of this book is adaptable, depending on the preferences and circumstances of the reader. (We do recommend, though, that parents still read through the book to know what their children are looking at and thinking about, and maybe talk with their child about some of the character traits from the book.) The "Action Activity" in each lesson can mostly be done alone, but you might want to invite a friend or family member to do it with you and talk about the topic when you do. And don't forget about the memory verses!

3. In a Sunday School Setting. The character traits, verses, and stories in this book can easily be adapted to be used in a class type of setting, either in a small group or in a Sunday school class or something similar. The selected verses are perfect to use as part of a verse memorization program, and the topics and questions can open up class discussion about the traits. The "Action Activity" can easily become a group activity, also opening up chances to talk about the "Hero Trait."

There are more ways and places it can be used, but those were just three ideas.

However this book is used, we hope that it opens up some of the stories in the Bible in a new way, and gets children and families thinking about how those stories and character traits and Bible verses can apply to our lives now.

GROWING UP

Hero: Jesus
Hero Trait: Growth
Key Verse: Luke 2:52
Story From: Luke 2:52

2,000 YEARS AGO A CHILD WAS BORN.

BUT THIS WAS NOT JUST ANY CHILD.

ANGELS ANNOUNCED HIS BIRTH.

A STAR LED SOME OF THE WORLD'S WISEST MEN TO HIS HOME.

A KING QUAKED IN FEAR THAT THIS CHILD WOULD TAKE HIS PLACE.

HE WAS A HUMAN, FLESH AND BLOOD.

BUT HE WAS ALSO GOD, PURE AND HOLY.

TIME PASSED, AND HE GREW.

FROM BABY TO TODDLER...

FROM TODDLER TO CHILD...

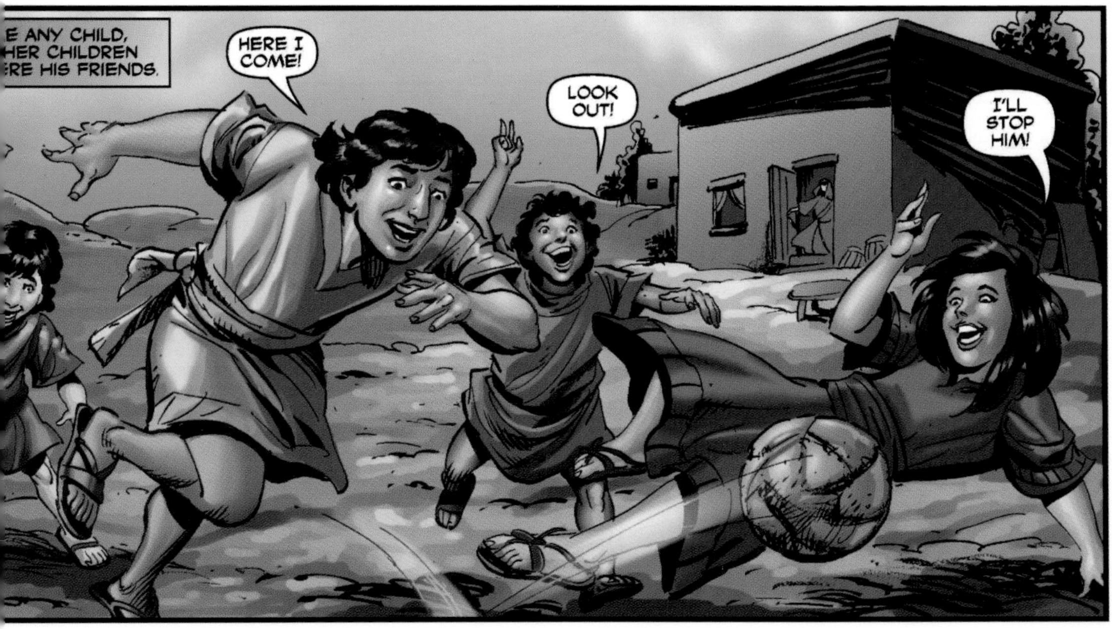
E ANY CHILD,
HER CHILDREN
ERE HIS FRIENDS.
HERE I COME!
LOOK OUT!
I'LL STOP HIM!

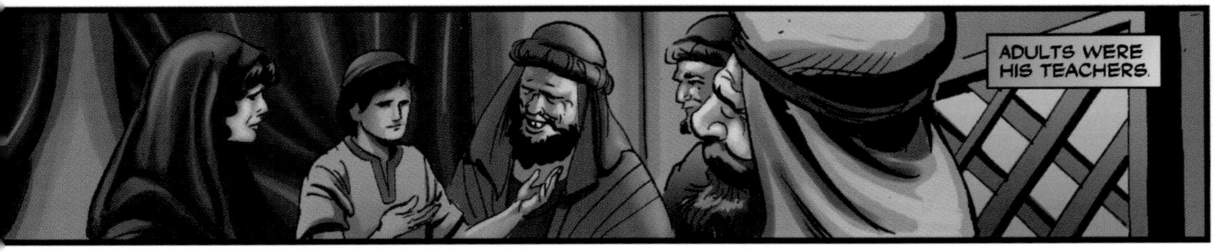
ADULTS WERE HIS TEACHERS.

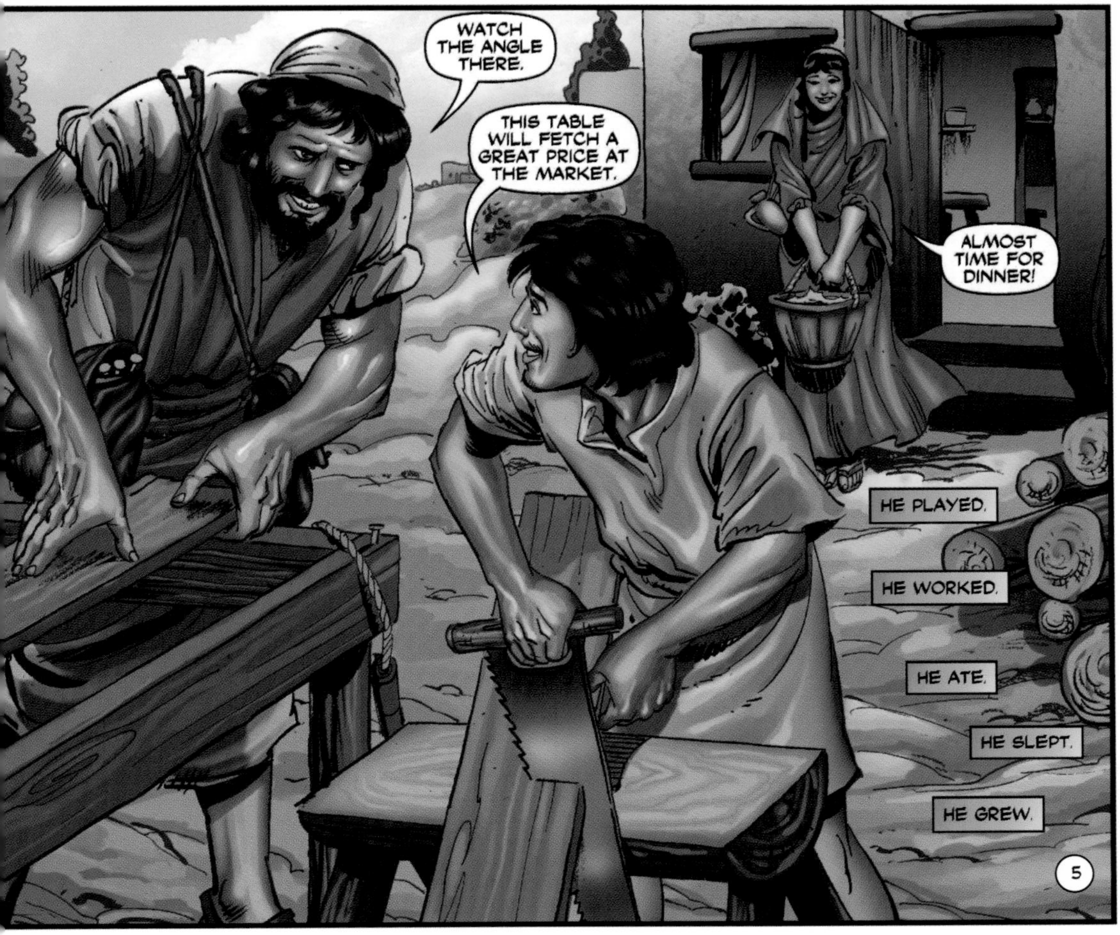
WATCH THE ANGLE THERE.
THIS TABLE WILL FETCH A GREAT PRICE AT THE MARKET.
ALMOST TIME FOR DINNER!
HE PLAYED.
HE WORKED.
HE ATE.
HE SLEPT.
HE GREW.

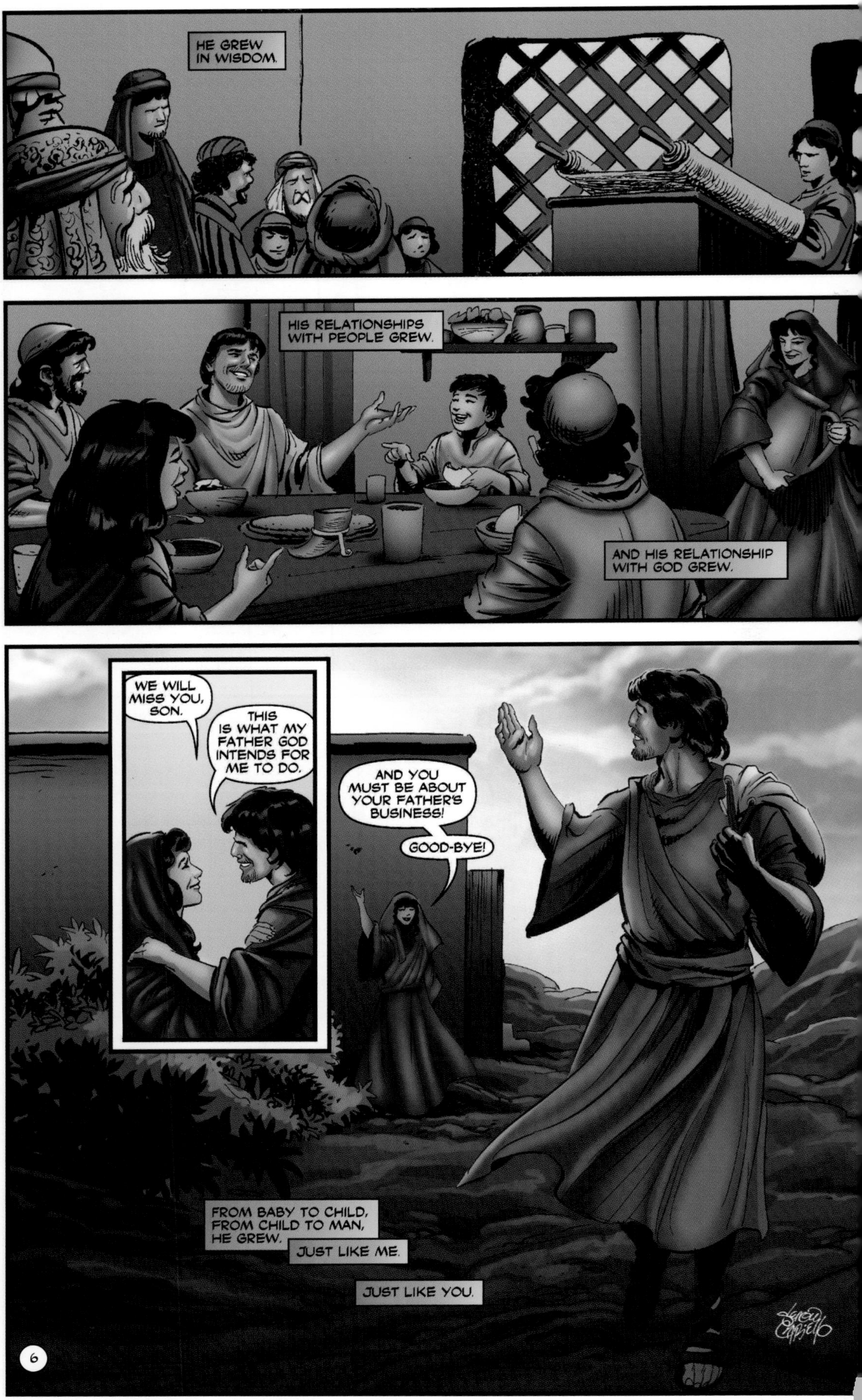
HE GREW IN WISDOM.
HIS RELATIONSHIPS WITH PEOPLE GREW.
AND HIS RELATIONSHIP WITH GOD GREW.
WE WILL MISS YOU, SON.
THIS IS WHAT MY FATHER GOD INTENDS FOR ME TO DO.
AND YOU MUST BE ABOUT YOUR FATHER'S BUSINESS!
GOOD-BYE!
FROM BABY TO CHILD, FROM CHILD TO MAN, HE GREW.
JUST LIKE ME.
JUST LIKE YOU.

Part Two:
"GROWTH"

GROWTH: *Changing and developing in a healthy way.*

Everything that lives grows. Trees grow upwards, reaching their branches to the sky. Caterpillars grow and change from creepy crawlies into winged wonders. Whales grow from enormous babies into even more enormous adults. And humans grow, from tiny, helpless children into strong men and women. Did you know that even though it looks like adults stop growing because they do not grow taller, some bones never stop growing? In the time it took to read this sentence, thousands of new cells in your body grew to replace old ones!

But humans grow in other ways, too, not just physically. As we get older, we also grow smarter. Just think about how many words a toddler knows and how many words a ten-year-old knows. When you were younger, you might have said something like this: "Mama! Mama! Mak!" Now, you say, "Hey, Mom, may I please have some milk?" In the years that have passed, your knowledge grew. You learned.

And we also grow spiritually. We learn the difference between right and wrong. We learn how to show love. We learn how to be good friends. We learn how to make good choices. When you were a baby, you probably bit people with your sharp, tiny teeth when they did something you didn't like. Now, you understand that hurting people is not a good thing to do, even when you're upset.

As we grow spiritually, we also learn about God. We learn about how much he loves us. We learn that he cares about how we act and the things we do. We learn that he wants to be our friend, both now and forever in heaven.

Growth is important for anything that is alive if it is going to stay healthy.

- Ask your mom or dad to tell you a story about some of the things you did when you were a baby that you do not do anymore. Ask them how you have changed since you were a baby.

- What would happen if you didn't grow? What would happen if you didn't learn?

Part Three:
"GROWTH" IN THE BIBLE

Luke 2:52 *And Jesus grew in wisdom and stature, and in favor with God and men.*

This verse describes four ways that Jesus grew.

He grew in wisdom. Wisdom is knowledge, but not just knowledge. It is using knowledge to make good choices.

He grew in stature. This means that Jesus' body grew. "Growing in stature" means taking care of a very special gift that God has given you: your body!

He grew in favor with God. That means that Jesus spent time studying the Bible and praying. Growing in favor with God means doing the things God wants you to do, and building your relationship with him.

He grew in favor with "man." This doesn't just mean men. It means with people, and that includes men and women, boys and girls. Jesus was someone that people liked to be around, because he treated people with kindness and friendliness.

- What does "growing in favor with people" mean in your life?
- What are some things you are already doing to grow in wisdom?
- What are some things you are already doing to grow in stature?

Part Four:

"GROWTH" IN THE STORY

This very short story in the Bible has a lot for us to learn. Jesus is the best example of how to live a life for God. In fact, if you are a Christian, here is something you should know about that word. Christian means "little Christ" or "Christ-like" or "follower of Christ." Being a Christian means you are like Jesus Christ.

So, being like Christ means that you are meant to grow.

You are meant to grow in wisdom.

You are meant to grow in stature.

You are meant to grow in favor with God.

You are meant to grow in favor with people.

Bugs, animals, plants, fish, birds, and people all have to grow to be healthy. A healthy body doesn't get sick as easily. An unhealthy body can't do all the things it needs to do.

Christians need to grow spiritually to be healthy, too. A healthy Christian can make good choices. A healthy Christian can treat people with kindness. A healthy Christian can fight temptation just like a healthy body fights sickness.

- How does this short story teach us to be like Jesus?

- If something does not grow, why does it become unhealthy?

Part Five:

"GROWTH" IN OUR LIVES

The rest of this book is about different ways we can grow. In the following chapters, you will learn about being a good friend. You will learn about being a Christian. You will learn about wisdom and where it comes from and what it is. You will learn about talking to God and listening to him. You will learn about many different traits that Christians should have.

Learning about these traits will help you grow. Learning about the stories will help you grow. Learning about and memorizing the verses in each lesson will help you grow.

We hope you have fun with these stories. We hope you learn from the verses. We hope the questions make you think.

But most of all, we hope reading this book helps you grow into the hero God meant for you to be!

• What are some things you can do to grow in wisdom?

• What are some things you can do to grow in favor with God?

ACTION ACTIVITY: GROWTH

Get some lima beans and put them in a zip-style plastic sandwich bag or freezer bag. Put some water in. Seal it. Put it near some sunlight. Then watch it sprout (almost) right before your eyes! You'll be surprised how quickly the bean will open and sprout. (It should do it within a day or two!) If you want, you can put the bean in dirt and watch it grow even bigger!

• What do plants need to grow?

• How are you like a growing plant?

THE BIG BOAT

Hero: Noah
Hero Trait: Diligence
Key Verse: Colossians 3:23
Story From: Genesis 6-8

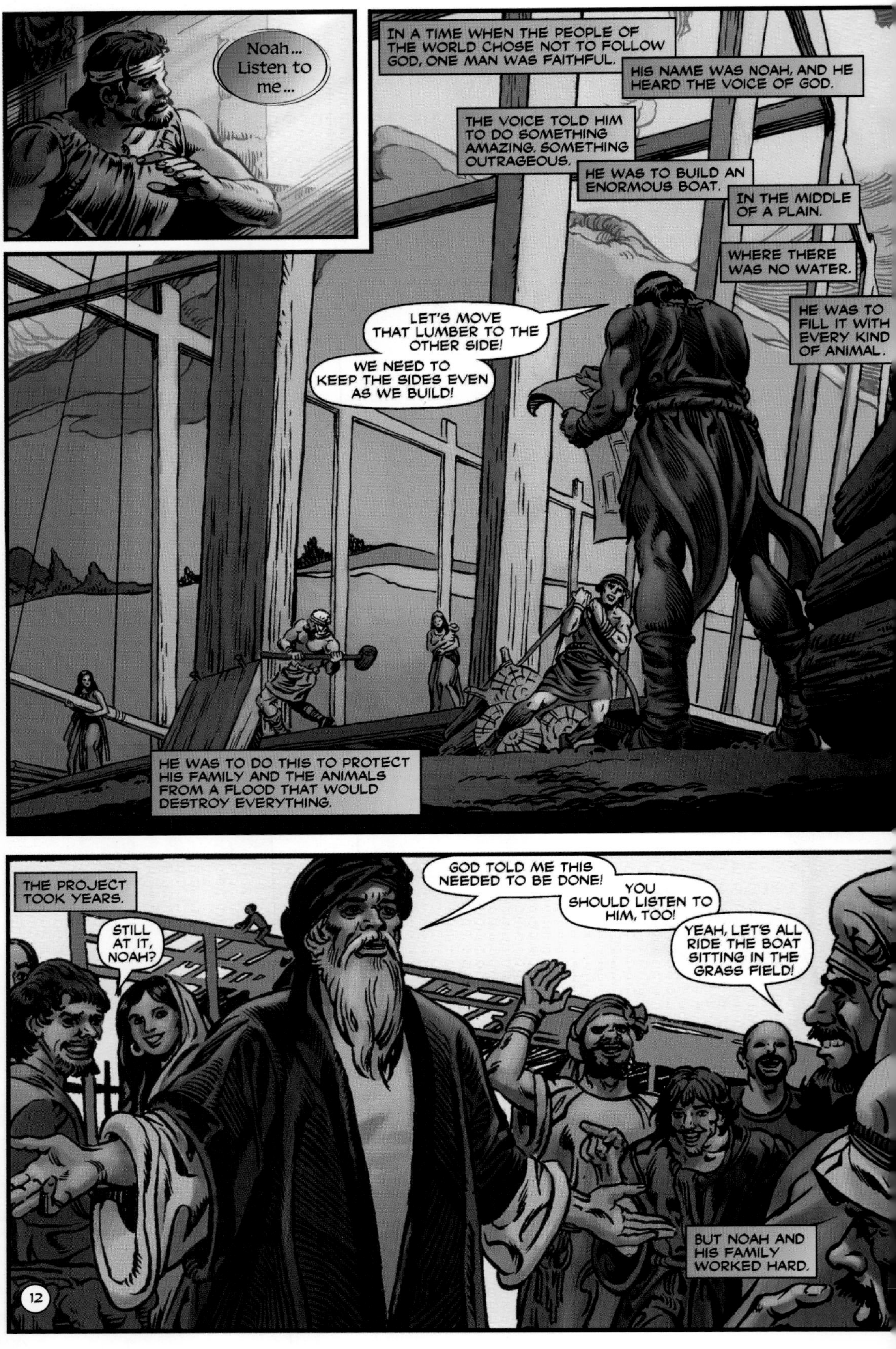
Noah... Listen to me...
IN A TIME WHEN THE PEOPLE OF THE WORLD CHOSE NOT TO FOLLOW GOD, ONE MAN WAS FAITHFUL.
HIS NAME WAS NOAH, AND HE HEARD THE VOICE OF GOD.
THE VOICE TOLD HIM TO DO SOMETHING AMAZING, SOMETHING OUTRAGEOUS.
HE WAS TO BUILD AN ENORMOUS BOAT.
IN THE MIDDLE OF A PLAIN.
WHERE THERE WAS NO WATER.
HE WAS TO FILL IT WITH EVERY KIND OF ANIMAL.
LET'S MOVE THAT LUMBER TO THE OTHER SIDE!
WE NEED TO KEEP THE SIDES EVEN AS WE BUILD!
HE WAS TO DO THIS TO PROTECT HIS FAMILY AND THE ANIMALS FROM A FLOOD THAT WOULD DESTROY EVERYTHING.
THE PROJECT TOOK YEARS.
STILL AT IT, NOAH?
GOD TOLD ME THIS NEEDED TO BE DONE!
YOU SHOULD LISTEN TO HIM, TOO!
YEAH, LET'S ALL RIDE THE BOAT SITTING IN THE GRASS FIELD!
BUT NOAH AND HIS FAMILY WORKED HARD.

FINALLY, IT WAS DONE!

JUST AS WAS PROMISED, THE ANIMALS CAME AND ENTERED THE BOAT.

WE'VE DONE WHAT WE WERE ASKED TO DO.

NOW, GOD IS DOING WHAT ONLY HE COULD DO.

AND IF THE ANIMALS ARE COMING, THEN THAT MEANS THE WATERS WILL BE COMING AS WELL!

WHEN THE ANIMALS WERE ABOARD, THE DOOR WAS CLOSED.

AND THE WATERS CAME.

AFTER FORTY DAYS OF RAIN, THE LAND WAS COVERED.

NOAH, HIS FAMILY, AND THE ANIMALS WERE KEPT SAFE.

DAYS TURNED TO WEEKS.

WEEKS TURNED TO MONTHS.

FINALLY, A BIRD WAS SENT OUT AND BROUGHT BACK A SIGN THAT THE WATERS WERE GETTING LOWER.

THE BOAT RAN AGROUND AS THE WATERS CONTINUED TO GO AWAY.

SOON, THE PEOPLE AND ANIMALS WERE ABLE TO LEAVE THE GREAT BOAT.

NOAH GAVE A SACRIFICE TO GOD.

A SACRIFICE OF PRAISE, OF THANKS, AND OF REMEMBRANCE.

GOD HAD PROMISED PROTECTION.

NOAH'S FAMILY WAS PROTECTED, BECAUSE THEY TRUSTED GOD AND WORKED HARD...

...FOR THEY KNEW THAT GOD WOULD DO WHAT HE PROMISED

Part Two:
"DILIGENCE"

DILIGENCE: *Doing your best work, especially to finish a job you have been given.*

Diligence is working hard on a job that you have been given to do. Diligence means that when you start something, you will work hard to finish it.

But finishing a job isn't the only goal when you are being diligent. Diligence also means doing your very best work. It means being careful to do the job right and to do the job well. If you are just trying to get the job done, and that is all you are thinking about, sometimes the work can be sloppy or the end result of the job is not good.

Diligence means giving your best effort to produce the best results.

- What would happen if no one in the world worked with diligence?

- Why do you think a boss who wants to hire someone for a job looks for a person who is diligent?

ACTION ACTIVITY: DILIGENCE

Build a house of cards using a regular deck of playing cards or UNO cards or whatever game you have available. Work hard, as a team, to use every single card in the deck (or half the deck, if you use UNO cards). (Look online for instructions showing how to do it if you aren't sure how.)

- Did you ever feel like giving up? Why or why not?

- What made finishing the job easy? What made finishing the job hard?

Part Three:
"DILIGENCE" IN THE BIBLE

Colossians 3:23 *Whatever you do, work at it with all your heart, as working for the Lord, not for men...*

This verse adds something to the way we think of doing work. This verse does not just say "do your best." It does not just say "be diligent." This verse says that when you do something, do it as if you were doing it for the Lord!

That changes how you look at your jobs a little bit, doesn't it? If you are cleaning your room, you're not just cleaning your room for Mom or Dad . . . you're cleaning if for the Lord.

You're not just helping a friend with yard work . . . you're doing it for the Lord.

Homework? It's not just for a grade. Not just for a teacher. Not just for your parents . . . it's for the Lord.

What does this mean? It means that you're not just doing your best so you look good. It's not just to make people happy. It's not just to get the job done so you can do something else. It means you are thinking about what God thinks about what you're doing.

• How does doing a job "for the Lord" change how you think about the different things you do?

• Does this verse mean that everything you do must be perfect? Why or why not?

Part Four:

"DILIGENCE" IN THE STORY

Noah was given a BIG job! Can you imagine being given the job to build a boat that is longer than a football field?

But the job came from God. God asked Noah to build the boat. And Noah worked diligently.

Why did Noah work with diligence? Well, for many reasons. He did it to make sure his family was safe. If you are building a boat and you are not careful, the boat might not float! Staying dry -- and alive -- is one good reason to work with diligence!

But another reason Noah worked with diligence is that God gave him the job. Noah did not have to do it, but he served and trusted God. So when God asked Noah to do it, he did it. It took him many years to finish, but he worked hard. When it was done, the boat floated and kept everyone and everything inside dry and safe.

The verse says to work "as though you were doing it for the Lord." Whenever we have a task to do, we can remember the example Noah set for us.

- What are some things that would have made Noah's job hard to do?

- How do you think Noah could remind himself to work with diligence?

Part Five:

"DILIGENCE" IN OUR LIVES

You're probably never going to be asked to build a boat. Especially a boat bigger than your house! But even though homework or chores won't protect your family from a deadly flood and even though your homework will never be to build a floating zoo, it is important to be diligent.

Every day, you have to do many different things. You may have to practice baseball or piano. You may have to write a report or figure out math problems. You may have to clean a garage or fold laundry. You may have to help cook dinner or wash the dirty dishes.

So, whether you are working or playing, how can you "do it as if you are doing it for the Lord?"

One thing that helps is to remember that everything you have is actually from the Lord. So when you are asked to help with laundry, remember that those clothes are a gift from God. And when your mom asks you to do dishes, remember that those dishes are a gift from the Lord! And even remember that your mom is a gift from the Lord!

- Just be diligent in whatever you do, because you are doing it for the Lord.

- What are some things that make it hard to do a job with diligence?

- What can you do to help remind you to "work as if you are doing it for the Lord"?

THE STINKIEST
TIME-OUT EVER

Hero: Jonah
Hero Trait: Teachability
Key Verse: Proverbs 12:1
Story From: Jonah

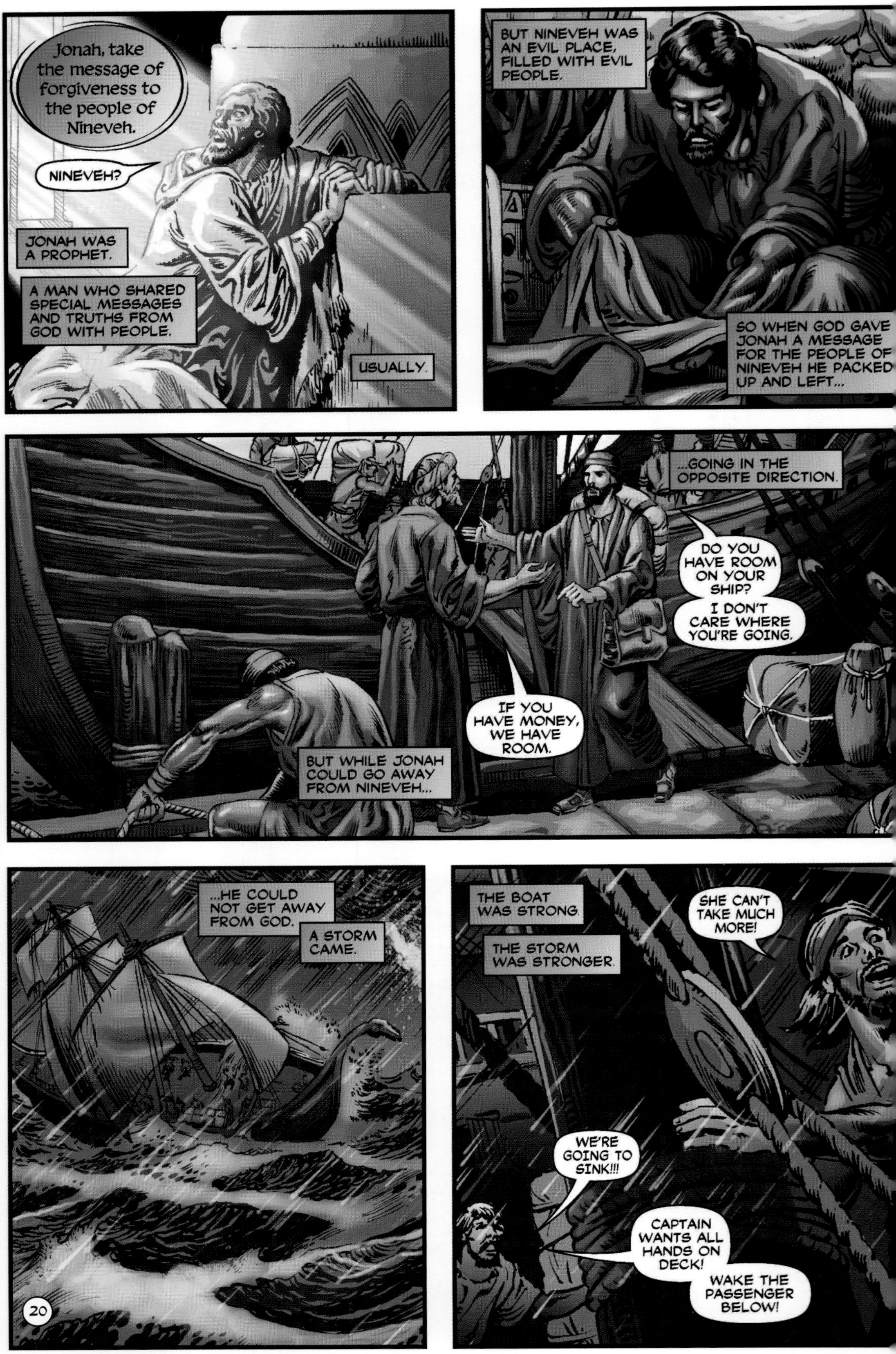
Jonah, take the message of forgiveness to the people of Nineveh.
NINEVEH?
JONAH WAS A PROPHET.
A MAN WHO SHARED SPECIAL MESSAGES AND TRUTHS FROM GOD WITH PEOPLE.
USUALLY.
BUT NINEVEH WAS AN EVIL PLACE, FILLED WITH EVIL PEOPLE.
SO WHEN GOD GAVE JONAH A MESSAGE FOR THE PEOPLE OF NINEVEH HE PACKED UP AND LEFT...
...GOING IN THE OPPOSITE DIRECTION.
DO YOU HAVE ROOM ON YOUR SHIP?
I DON'T CARE WHERE YOU'RE GOING.
IF YOU HAVE MONEY, WE HAVE ROOM.
BUT WHILE JONAH COULD GO AWAY FROM NINEVEH...
...HE COULD NOT GET AWAY FROM GOD.
A STORM CAME.
THE BOAT WAS STRONG.
THE STORM WAS STRONGER.
SHE CAN'T TAKE MUCH MORE!
WE'RE GOING TO SINK!!!
CAPTAIN WANTS ALL HANDS ON DECK!
WAKE THE PASSENGER BELOW!

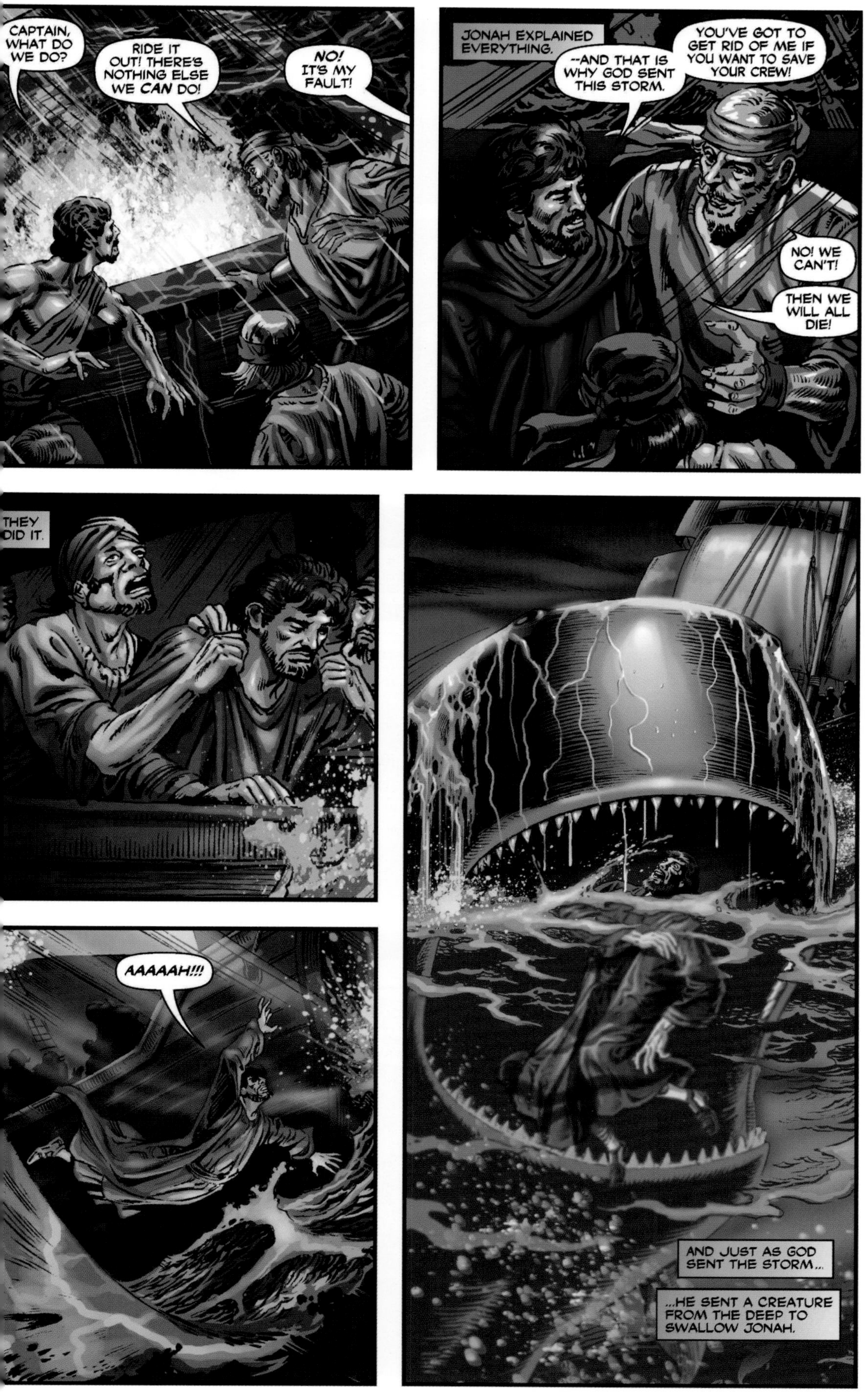
CAPTAIN, WHAT DO WE DO?
RIDE IT OUT! THERE'S NOTHING ELSE WE CAN DO!
NO! IT'S MY FAULT!
JONAH EXPLAINED EVERYTHING.
--AND THAT IS WHY GOD SENT THIS STORM.
YOU'VE GOT TO GET RID OF ME IF YOU WANT TO SAVE YOUR CREW!
NO! WE CAN'T!
THEN WE WILL ALL DIE!
THEY DID IT.
AAAAAH!!!
AND JUST AS GOD SENT THE STORM...
...HE SENT A CREATURE FROM THE DEEP TO SWALLOW JONAH.

JONAH LIVED THE NEXT THREE DAYS IN THE BELLY OF THE BEAST.

HE HAD TIME TO THINK.

LISTEN.

PRAY.

LEARN.

YOU ASKED ME TO TAKE YOUR MESSAGE OF FORGIVENESS TO NINEVEH.

BUT IT IS I WHO NEEDS FORGIVENESS.

I SHOULD NOT HAVE R... THOSE PEOP... NEED YOU... MESSAGE.

THE SEA CREATURE VOMITED JONAH UP.

AS SOON AS HE WAS ON DRY LAND, HE WENT TO NINEVEH.

HE GAVE THEM GOD'S MESSAGE.

YOU HAVE GONE YOUR OWN WAY, AND IGNORED GOD'S WAY!

GOD WILL SEND HIS PUNISHMENT FOR THAT.

BUT HE WILL ALSO GIVE FORGIVENESS AND MERCY!

I HAVE LEARNED THIS MYSELF RECENTLY!

Part Two:
"TEACHABILITY"

TEACHABILITY: *Being willing to learn, especially from lessons, consequences, and correcting mistakes.*

Teachability is a pretty easy word to define. It is the ability to be taught. It means if someone is trying to teach you something, you let them teach you and you let yourself learn from them.

Sometimes people use this word when they are talking about learning in school. Sometimes it is about learning a sport or a musical instrument. Someone who is teachable listens closely to the lesson and practices what they have been taught.

A teachable person listens to lessons about how they should treat other people, how they should act, or the things they should or should not do. It means allowing someone to correct you.

A teachable person allows someone to correct them. This correction comes in different ways, but the purpose of correction is always the same: taking something that is wrong and correcting it to make it right.

Sometimes a correction may just be words. For example, if you lie about your homework, you might be told, "Do not lie to me, because I will not know when I can trust you." You can learn from that.

Sometimes a correction involves a punishment of some sort. For example, if you hurt your brother or sister, you may lose a privilege or get sent to time-out.

And sometimes a correction comes from what are called "natural consequences." For example, if you get mad and kick a wall, you will hurt your foot.

If you are teachable, you will learn the lessons that each of those situations can teach you.

- What are some ways words can teach you?

- Think of another example for natural consequences. How could that teach you a lesson?

Part Three:
"TEACHABILITY" IN THE BIBLE

Proverbs 12:1 *Whoever loves discipline loves knowledge, but he who hates correction is stupid.*

There are some strong words in this verse!

What is this verse trying to say? Does it mean we're stupid if we don't like to be punished? Not at all. Most people don't like to be punished. Being punished does not feel good.

Instead, this verse means that punishments and corrections are meant to teach you a lesson. And if you learn from those lessons, good can come from it. When your mom or dad gets a speeding ticket for going too fast, they have to pay a fine. They probably don't like paying that fine, but that fine helps them remember next time they are driving to go the speed limit.

If you are in math class and you get a problem wrong, but do not listen to the teacher when she or he shows you how to do it, you will not learn how to do the problem correctly.

The same is true for our spirit. If you tell lies, you need to learn not to do that. If you fight with your brothers or sisters, you need to learn not to do that. If you "love discipline", that means you are willing to learn from your mistakes. You are willing to learn from the times you are told how to do things. And, yes, you are willing to learn from the punishments you get. If you "hate correction", you keep doing things wrong and ignore what your parents and teachers are trying to teach you.

- What is a punishment you can remember that really helped you learn a lesson?

- Why is it hard to learn a lesson from a punishment?

24

Part Four:
"TEACHABILITY" IN THE STORY

Jonah was given a job. God told him exactly what he needed to do, but Jonah disobeyed. He decided he did not want to do what God told him to do. Not only did he choose to disobey God, he decided to go in the opposite direction!

So God put him in time-out. In a fish's stomach. (Kind of makes you appreciate just being sent to your room, doesn't it?)

God could have easily sent someone else. He could have let Jonah run away and never bothered with Jonah again. But God wanted Jonah to learn his lesson. God gave Jonah a chance to learn from his mistake.

And Jonah did. Jonah was being teachable. He probably did not like the time he spent in the fish's belly, but he learned from it.

- What was the lesson Jonah learned?

- How was Jonah being "teachable"?

ACTION ACTIVITY: TEACHABILITY

Get a maze (it could be from a book or a website, or you could even make your own by searching for "maze maker" online) and make a copy of it, but don't look too closely at it. Time yourself while you do the maze. Now, get the copy you made of that same maze and time yourself while you do it again.

- Did what you learned about the maze the first time help you when you did it the second time?

- How can we be teachable when we learn from experience (like you did with the maze)?

- What are some other ways to learn and be teachable?

Part Five:

"TEACHABILITY"
IN OUR LIVES

Are you "teachable"? Do you try to learn from your mistakes? Do you try to learn from the consequences of your actions?

Getting a punishment or a consequence is hard, because there are a lot of emotions involved. Sometimes your mom or dad is angry when they give you the punishment. And when they are angry, you can feel sad or mad yourself. Sometimes you can feel embarrassed that people know you did something wrong. Sometimes, if you did something wrong because you were mad or upset, you still have those feelings when you get corrected. And when you have to go through the consequences -- whether it is doing something you don't want or losing something you do want -- you can feel mad or sad, too.

But after all those emotions have settled down, hopefully you are able to understand a new lesson. If you chose to lie and got a consequence, hopefully the next time you are tempted to lie, you will remember that consequence. But after all those emotions have settled down, hopefully you will have learned a new lesson.

Being teachable means you are willing to learn. It means you want to be a better person and you want to be more like Jesus, so you want to learn.

- When an adult who loves you gives you a punishment or a consequence for doing something wrong or bad, how does that make you feel?

- How can they actually be showing love to you?

EARTH, WIND, FIRE...
AND WHISPERS

Hero: Elijah
Hero Trait: Attentiveness
Key Verse: John 10:27
Story From: I Kings 19

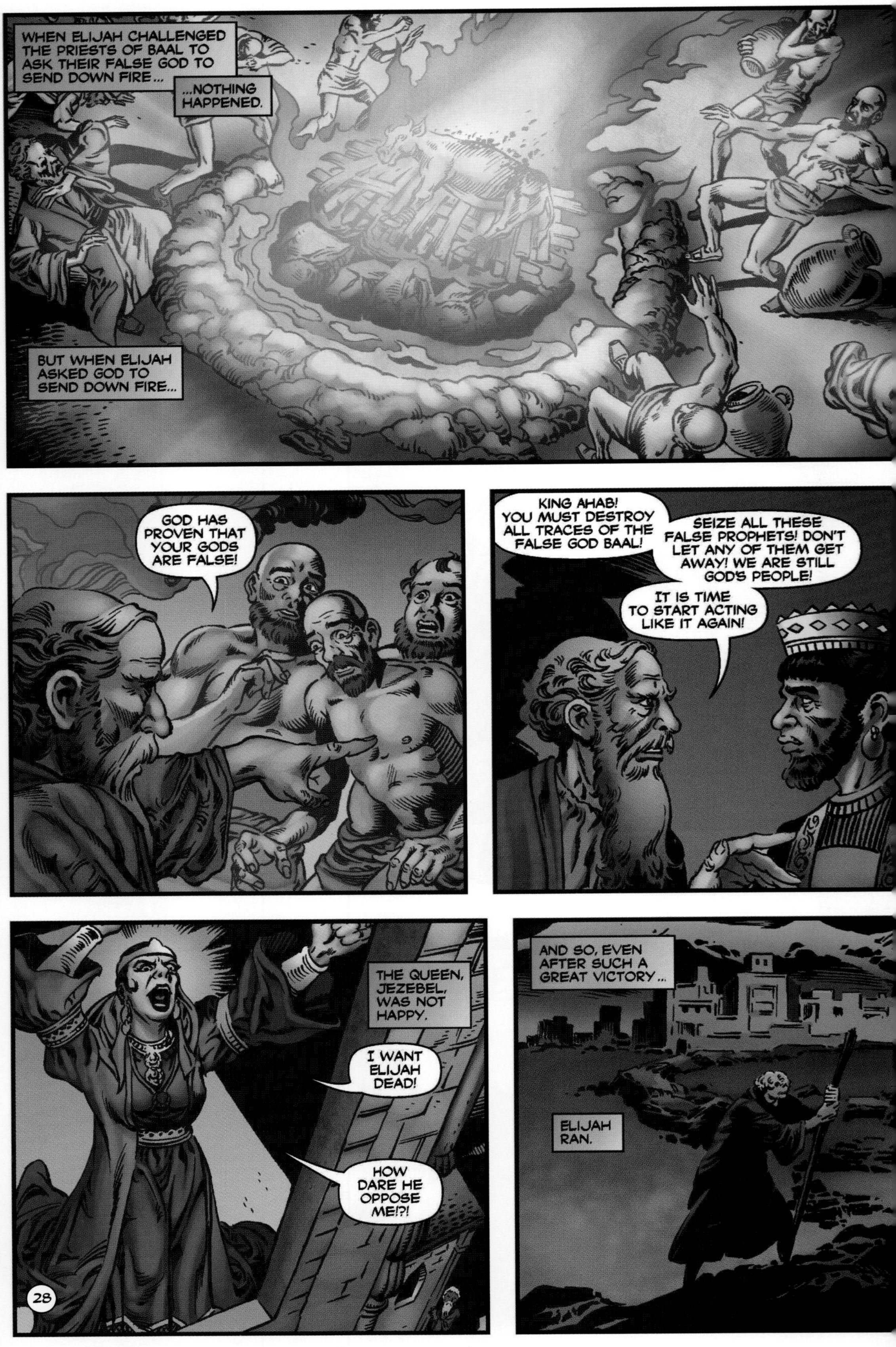
WHEN ELIJAH CHALLENGED THE PRIESTS OF BAAL TO ASK THEIR FALSE GOD TO SEND DOWN FIRE...
...NOTHING HAPPENED.
BUT WHEN ELIJAH ASKED GOD TO SEND DOWN FIRE...
GOD HAS PROVEN THAT YOUR GODS ARE FALSE!
KING AHAB! YOU MUST DESTROY ALL TRACES OF THE FALSE GOD BAAL!
SEIZE ALL THESE FALSE PROPHETS! DON'T LET ANY OF THEM GET AWAY! WE ARE STILL GOD'S PEOPLE!
IT IS TIME TO START ACTING LIKE IT AGAIN!
THE QUEEN, JEZEBEL, WAS NOT HAPPY.
I WANT ELIJAH DEAD!
HOW DARE HE OPPOSE ME!?!
AND SO, EVEN AFTER SUCH A GREAT VICTORY...
ELIJAH RAN.

AFTER HE RAN FOR A WHILE, HE HEARD THE LORD SPEAK TO HIM.

What are you doing, Elijah?

LORD, I'VE FAITHFULLY SERVED YOU.

BUT THE PEOPLE OF ISRAEL *AREN'T* SERVING YOU ANYMORE!

THEY'VE EVEN DESTROYED THE PLACES OF WORSHIP.

AND THEY'VE KILLED YOUR PROPHETS!

I'M THE LAST ONE LEFT.

NOW THEY'RE TRYING TO KILL ME.

Go, stand on the mountain.

The presence of the Lord is going to pass by ...

ELIJAH DID AS HE WAS TOLD. WHAT AWESOME FORM WOULD THE LORD'S PRESENCE TAKE?

A POWERFUL WIND CAME, BATTERING THE ROCKS! BUT THE LORD WAS NOT IN THE WIND.

A MIGHTY EARTHQUAKE CAME, SHAKING THE MOUNTAIN! BUT THE LORD WAS NOT IN THE EARTHQUAKE.

A GREAT FIRE CAME, CONSUMING THE TREES! BUT THE LORD WAS NOT IN THE FIRE.

A GENTLE WHISPER CAME, BARELY TICKLING ELIJAH'S EARS.

What are you doing, Elijah?

THE SMOKE CLEARED, THE DUST SETTLED, THE WIND DIED DOWN, AND ELIJAH ANSWERED GOD'S QUESTION...

LORD, I'V[E] FAITHFULL[Y] SERVED YO[U]

BUT THE PEOPLE OF ISRAEL N[O] LONGER D[O]

THEY'VE EVEN DESTROYED THE PLACES OF WORSHIP AND YOUR PROPHETS!

NOW, I'M THE LAST ONE LEFT AND THEY'RE TRYING TO KILL ME.

Go back, Elijah.

You will anoint a new king of Aram and a new king of Israel.

You will find Elisha, son of Shaphat, to take your place as my prophet.

You feel alone, but you are not.

There are seven thousand people who have not bowed to the false god Baal.

And I am with you.

ELIJAH LISTENED TO WHAT GOD SAID. HE STOPPED RUNNIN[G] IN FEAR, CHOOSING T[O] FOLLOW GOD INSTEA[D]

30

Part Two:
"ATTENTIVENESS"

Attentiveness: *Being a good listener and giving your full attention to people, to tasks, and to God.*

Attentiveness is when you pay careful attention. It means you are giving someone your complete concentration. When you are attentive, you are showing that a person or a thing is important to you.

It means showing you care about someone by caring about what they are saying. It means you are aware not just of the words someone is saying, but also you are aware of why they are saying these things, how they are feeling, and what they need or want. Someone who is attentive is a respectful listener.

There are many different people we should be attentive to. We should show attentiveness to our parents, to our teachers, and to our friends. We should show attentiveness to people who are taking care of us and to people who are trying to communicate with us.

And, most importantly, we should show attentiveness to God.

- What are some times when you need to work extra hard to be attentive?
- Who are some people you should show attentiveness to?
- Why should you be attentive to God?

Part Three:
"ATTENTIVENESS" IN THE BIBLE

John 10:27 My sheep listen to my voice; I know them, and they follow me.

Think about sheep and their shepherd. The shepherd takes care of them. The shepherd leads them from place to place so they can find food, water, and safety. The sheep listen to their shepherd and learn to hear his voice. If someone else calls them, they do not follow that voice. They follow the voice of their shepherd, because they know their shepherd wants to keep them safe.

This is why we need to be attentive and listen for God's voice. God speaks to us. He uses many different ways to speak to us. Sometimes he uses people like our parents and preachers and teachers at church. Sometimes he uses the Bible. Sometimes he uses feelings. Sometimes he uses something we see or hear.

But he does speak to us.

What does he speak to us about? Listening to him helps us know what is right and what is wrong. Listening to him helps us make tough choices. Listening to him helps us, just like the verse says, follow him.

- If we are like sheep, how is God like a shepherd?
- What could happen to a sheep that does not listen to the shepherd?

ACTION ACTIVITY: ATTENTIVENESS

Play the telephone game. (The more people the better!) The first person whispers a sentence to the second person, who whispers it to the third person, who whispers it to the fourth person, and so on. The last person says it for everyone to hear, and then the first person reveals the original sentence. The end result may be funny or may amaze you because it is perfect. But for the phrase to get from one end to the other, you have to be attentive.

- What makes this game easy? What makes it hard?

Part Four:
"ATTENTIVENESS" IN THE STORY

Elijah had an exciting and interesting life. And sometimes it was also very scary.

He was the man who prayed for God to send fire down from heaven in a contest with people who worshipped their false god Baal. Those Baal worshippers asked their god, Baal, to send down fire and nothing happened, because Baal was not real and had no power. But Elijah worshipped God, who was real and who did have power. And God showed it!

But after that, the queen wanted Elijah dead! So he ran away and hid. Imagine that! After God did such an amazing thing, Elijah ran away in fear.

While he was hiding, he wanted to hear what God had to say to him. He was told to listen from a cave on Mount Sinai. There was an awesome fire! A loud earthquake! A mighty wind! But God did not choose to speak to Elijah through any of those things.

Instead, God spoke to Elijah in a whisper. Why? Maybe it was to remind Elijah to listen carefully. Maybe it was so Elijah could remember that God was right there, by his side. Maybe it was to show Elijah that God does not only speak in big, explosive ways.

And Elijah listened. He listened carefully. He heard the fire and the wind and the earthquake, and because he listened carefully he knew that was not how God was going to speak to him.

He listened carefully, and because he listened carefully he heard the whisper. And he heard what God had to say.

- Could God have used the fire or the earthquake or the wind to speak to Elijah?
- Why do you think God spoke to Elijah with a whisper?

Part Five:
"ATTENTIVENESS" IN OUR LIVES

There are many things that distract us. Think of all the electronic devices you use in a day. Video games, television, movies, the Internet, iThis and iThat . . . all competing for our time and our attention.

They are competing for our time with God. They are competing for our attention to God.

If we want to hear God's voice, we need to be listening. How do you listen to God?

God also speaks to us through godly men and women we may know. But if we do not spend time with them, we cannot hear what they have to say.

God speaks in many different ways. When we pray, when we talk to God, we sometimes hear him talk back. It may not be in a voice, or even a whisper. It may be a feeling or an idea, and when that happens we should talk to one of those godly friends who can help us understand what it means or if it really is from God. Or we should look in the Bible to see if it is something that goes along with God's word. But if we do not talk to God and spend quiet time with him in prayer, we will not be able to listen for him.

There are many other ways that God talks to us. But the important thing is that we must be like Elijah. If we want to hear what God has to say, we have to listen to him.

- What are some ways that we can listen to what God has to say to us?

- What are some things that get in the way of listening to God? How can we stop those distractions?

- What kind of things do you want to listen to God for?

34

THE GIRL WHO DIDN'T WANT TO BE QUEEN

Hero: Esther
Hero Trait: Availability
Key Verse: Isaiah 6:8
Story From: Esther

ESTHER LIVED A PEACEFUL LIFE, CARED FOR BY HER COUSIN MORDECAI.

THAT WOMAN!

THE KING NEEDS A NEW QUEEN

SHE IS PERFECT!

YOU WILL BE PRESENTED TO THE KING. WE WILL SEE WHAT HE THINKS.

SHE WAS BROUGHT BEFORE THE KING.

THE KING SAW HER BEAUTY.

I HAVE FOUND MY NEW QUEEN!

ESTHER ENTERED A NEW LIFE. A LIFE SHE NEVER WANTED.

A LIFE OF GREAT COMFORT, BUT ALSO A LIFE OF STRICT RULES.

A LIFE AWAY FROM HER PEOPLE AND FAMILY.

SHE WAS NOW THE QUEEN OF PERSIA-- THE NATION THAT MADE HER PEOPLE-- THE JEWS--SLAVES!

BUT SHE STILL COMMUNICATED WITH HER COUSIN, AND ONE DAY...

A MESSENGER IS HERE.

36

A MESSAGE FROM MORDECAI, MY QUEEN.

HE SITS AT THE GATES, IN MOURNING.

WHAT'S WRONG?

ONE OF THE KING'S MEN HAMAN, HAS TRICKED THE KING INTO SIGNING A LAW THAT COULD KILL THE JEWS

GO! ASK MORDE WHAT CAN D

SOON AFTER.

WHAT DID HE SAY?

HE SAID THAT YOU, AS THE KING'S WIFE, ARE THE ONLY ONE WHO CAN TALK TO THE KING ABOUT HAMAN.

YOU MUST GO TO THE KING AND SPEAK FOR YOUR PEOPLE.

BUT I CAN'T! TO GO BEFORE THE KING WITHOUT BEING SUMMONED MEANS DEATH, UNLESS HE EXTENDS HIS SCEPTOR!

IT IS TOO DANGEROUS! I CAN'T...

MORDECAI SAYS YOU MAY HAVE BEEN PUT IN THIS PLACE FOR A TIME LIKE THIS.

HE'S RIGHT, OF COURSE. GOD PUT ME HERE. I NEED TO BE AVAILABLE TO DO WHAT NEEDS TO BE DONE.

TELL MORDECAI TO ASK OUR PEOPLE TO PRAY FOR ME. I WILL DO IT.

AT THE THRONE ROOM.

I AM HERE TO SEE THE KING.

BUT YOU COULD BE KILLED IF HE DOES NOT ACCEPT YOU!

I KNOW.

MY QUEEN WISHES TO SEE ME?

LET HER IN!

OH GOOD!

WHAT BRINGS YOU HERE?

A REQUEST, MY HUSBAND.

NAME IT. ANYTHING FOR YOU.

PLEASE, LET ME MAKE DINNER FOR YOU...AND FOR HAMAN.

37

ESTHER PREPARED THE DINNER FOR THE KING AND FOR HAMAN...THE MAN WHO WOULD KILL HER PEOPLE. AT THIS FIRST DINNER, SHE DID NOTHING. IT WAS A PLEASANT MEAL, AND WHEN IT WAS OVER, SHE INVITED THEM TO ANOTHER.

THANK YOU FOR COMING AGAIN.

IT IS AN HONOR TO DINE WITH MY KING AND QUEEN!

AT THE SECOND MEAL ...

ESTHER, MY QUEEN, ASK ME FOR ANYTHING!

EVEN HALF MY KINGDOM!

WHATEVER YOU WANT, I'LL GIVE YOU!

I JUST WANT MY PEOPLE TO B RESCUED.

SOMEONE HAS PLOTTED TO MURDER MY PEOPLE!

WHAT? OUTRAGEOUS!

WHO? WHO IS IT?

I WILL DESTROY HIM!!!

THIS MAN, RIGHT HERE!

HAMAN, THE ENEMY OF MY PEOPLE!

HE TRICKED YOU INTO SIGNIN A LAW TO DESTRO MY PEOPLE!

YOU WANT ME TO DESTR MY QUEEN'S PEOPLE? INSTEAD, I WILL DESTR YOU!

THIS WIL BE FIXE ESTHE!

STARTING WITH HIM!

A NEW LAW WAS SIGNED BY THE KING.

A LAW THAT PROTECTED ESTHER'S PEOPLE.

ALL BECAUSE ESTHER WAS AVAILABLE TO DO WHAT NEEDED TO BE DONE.

38

Part Two:

"AVAILABILITY"

Availability: *Being ready and willing to do what needs to be done, when it needs to be done.*

Sometimes, when you watch a commercial, you might hear a quick, low voice say at the end of the commercial, "Available for a limited time." What does that mean?

It means that whatever that commercial is talking about will not be around forever. You can only get it for a short time.

But if you are someone who is following God, you cannot be "available for a limited time." You need to be ready for what God has planned for you at all times.

Availability means you are ready to serve. It means that you are ready to do what needs to be done when you are asked. It means changing your own plans when you see that God has something else planned for you. It might even mean changing the things you want so they line up with the things God wants.

God wants us to be available, so we can be a part of his great, special plan for our lives and for his great, special plan for the lives of the people around us.

- Other than God, who are some people you should show "availability" to?
- What can happen when you are not available for something important?

Part Three:
"AVAILABILITY" IN THE BIBLE

Isaiah 6:8 Then I heard the voice of the Lord saying, "Whom shall I send? And who will go for us?" And I said, "Here am I. Send me!"

This Bible verse comes from the story of a man named Isaiah. Isaiah was in a special place where he could see angels and could hear the voice of God. God was looking for someone to take a message to the people in Israel when he asked, "Whom shall I send and who will go for us?"

Isaiah's answer is the same answer we should give when God wants us to do something. "Here I am, send me!"

There are many different people in the Bible who had to change their plans because God asked them to do something they never expected. You probably know some people in your own family or in your church that changed their plans when God asked them to do something. (You should ask around. You'll hear some interesting stories!)

Availability means when God asks you to do something, your answer is, "Yes! Here I am! Send me!"

- How can you know if God is asking you to do something?

- What does it mean to say, "Here I am, send me," to God?

ACTION ACTIVITY: AVAILABILITY

Get a light weight ball or crumple up some paper into some balls (don't crumple them too small, though). Find a partner and toss the ball back and forth five times. Now, toss the ball back and forth five times again, but this time whoever is catching the ball has to cross their arms and try to catch it that way!

- How would it feel if you were trying to win a game and your partner crossed their arms like that?

- How is this game like being available to something God wants you to do?

Part Four:
"AVAILABILITY"
IN THE STORY

Esther was just a young woman who wanted to have a normal life. She was not looking for fame or fortune. She surely did not think she would be queen.

But it happened. She was taken away from her friends and family and put in a strange place, away from everything she knew. It was comfortable. It was luxurious. But it was not home. She probably thought that missing her cousin and being homesick was as difficult as things were going to get.

She was wrong. She found out about a plan to kill her friends and family and all the people from her country. And she was the only person who could do something about it. She was the only person who could ask the king for help, and the king was the only person who could help. But going to the king was dangerous. She did not want to do it.

Then, after some encouragement from her cousin, just like Isaiah in the verse, she said she would go where she was sent. She put aside her plans and her comfortable life and she made herself available. And her people were saved because of it.

- Esther was in a dangerous situation when she went to the king. Why do you think she did it?

- What kind of feelings do you think she felt when she was deciding what to do and getting ready to do it?

Part Five:

"AVAILABILITY" IN OUR LIVES

Someone who is available is a servant. If you are available, you are ready to serve. If you are available to someone else, you will put the things they want first, so when they call on you, you are ready to jump into action.

Availability means you are listening for what God wants you to do.

God wants us to help other people, so being available means watching for ways to help other people, too.

God wants us to tell other people about him, so being available means listening to your friends and looking for good times to talk about him with them.

God wants us to use the talents and abilities he gave us, so being available means looking for ways to help people in a special way that only we can.

There are many other ways you can be available. Availability means being ready to serve God, so keep your eyes and ears and mind open and be ready for when it's time for you to say, "Here I am, send me!"

- What are some situations when you might need to put someone else first and not do what you want so you can serve them?

- What kind of talents or abilities do you have? How can you be ready to use them to serve God or to serve other people?

THE VEGETABLE TEST

Hero: Shadrach, Meshach, & Abednego
(part 1 of 3)
Hero Trait: Friendship
Key Verse: Ecclesiastes 4:12
Story From: Daniel 1:1-21

IT WAS A DARK TIME FOR THE PEOPLE OF ISRAEL.

THE KINGDOM OF BABYLON RULED OVER THEM, AND TOOK MANY OF THEIR PEOPLE AS SLAVES OR PRISONERS.

SOME OF THEM--THE SMARTEST YOUNG MEN-- WERE TAKEN TO SERVE IN THE KING'S PALACE.

YOU ARE THE BRIGHTEST YOUNG MEN IN THE LAND.

WE WILL TEACH YOU HOW TO GIVE THE KING WISE ADVICE.

IF YOU DO WELL, YOU WILL BECOME TRUSTED OFFICIALS OUR GOVERNMENT.

IN THAT GROUP WERE FOUR FRIENDS.

SHADRACH.

MESHACH.

DANIEL.

ABEDNEGO.

WOW, LOOK AT THIS PLACE!

THIS IS NOTHING LIKE HOME.

BUT WE MUST STAND TOGETHER AND NOT FORGET OUR HOME.

YES, WE MUST REMEMBE WHAT WE HAV BEEN TAUGH

IN THE PALACES OF BABYLON, THEY STARTED THEIR TRAINING.

BUT ALMOST AT THE VERY BEGINNING THEY FACED A CHALLENGE.

IT WAS NOT A PROBLEM FOR THE OTHERS.

BUT TO THEM...

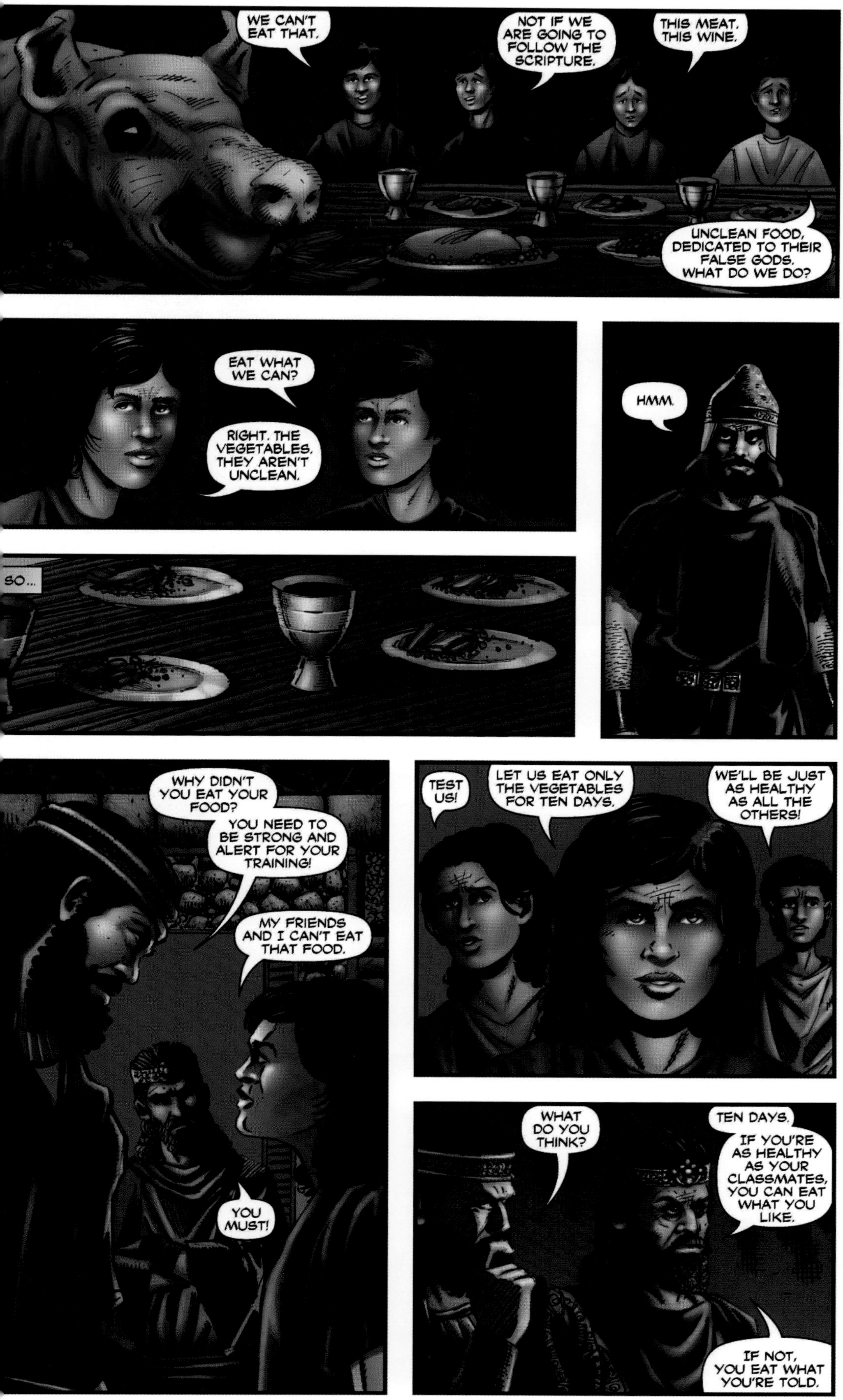
WE CAN'T EAT THAT.
NOT IF WE ARE GOING TO FOLLOW THE SCRIPTURE.
THIS MEAT. THIS WINE.
UNCLEAN FOOD, DEDICATED TO THEIR FALSE GODS. WHAT DO WE DO?
EAT WHAT WE CAN?
RIGHT. THE VEGETABLES. THEY AREN'T UNCLEAN.
SO...
HMM.
WHY DIDN'T YOU EAT YOUR FOOD?
YOU NEED TO BE STRONG AND ALERT FOR YOUR TRAINING!
MY FRIENDS AND I CAN'T EAT THAT FOOD.
YOU MUST!
TEST US!
LET US EAT ONLY THE VEGETABLES FOR TEN DAYS.
WE'LL BE JUST AS HEALTHY AS ALL THE OTHERS!
WHAT DO YOU THINK?
TEN DAYS.
IF YOU'RE AS HEALTHY AS YOUR CLASSMATES, YOU CAN EAT WHAT YOU LIKE.
IF NOT, YOU EAT WHAT YOU'RE TOLD.

TEN DAYS LATER.

SO, IT'S BEEN TEN DAYS.

YOU FOUR BOYS HAVE STUCK TOGETHER AND NOT EATEN ANY OF OUR MEAT OR HAD ANY OF OUR WINE.

WE'VE TESTED YOU AND YOU ARE *NOT* AS HEALTHY AS THE OTHERS.

YOU'RE *MORE* HEALTHY!

YOU HAVE SURPRISED US ALL!

WE WEREN'T SURPRISED!

WE KNEW THAT IF WE WERE FAITHFUL TO OUR GOD, HE WOULD BE FAITHFUL TO US!

WILL YOU STICK TO OUR DEAL?

MAYBE YOU SHOULD MAKE EVERYONE EAT OUR DIET!

I DON'T KNOW ABOUT THAT.

I DO KNOW WHEN I AM DEFEATED, THOUGH.

YOU WILL ONLY BE SERVED VEGETABLES, YES.

YOU STOOD TOGETHER, AND YOU SUCCEEDED!

THANK YOU FOR GIVING US THE CHANCE TO PROVE OURSELVES.

DANIEL AND HIS FRIENDS IMPRESSED EVERYONE IN THE KING'S COURT, SURPASSING THEIR MANY CLASSMATES.

TOGETHER, THEY STAYED FAITHFUL TO GOD.

AND TOGETHER THEY WER[E] PROMOTED INTO HIGHER AND HIGHER POSITIONS IN THE GOVERNMENT.

46

Part Two:
"FRIENDSHIP"

FRIENDSHIP: *Having positive relationships with people who encourage and help each other.*

When you think of the most important people in your life, you probably think of two groups of people: family and friends. Why are friends so important?

Maybe a better question is why is it so important to have GOOD friends? And why is it important to BE a good friend?

Think about what a GOOD friend does. A good friend is someone who encourages. Someone who helps. Someone who supports.

A good friend is someone who wants to see you grow closer to God. Someone who wants to help you make good choices. Someone who wants to help you up when you're feeling down, or support you when things aren't going your way.

- Why is it so important to have GOOD friends?
- Why is it important to BE a good friend?

Part Three:
"FRIENDSHIP" IN THE BIBLE

Ecclesiastes 4:12 Though one may be overpowered, two can defend themselves A cord of three strands is not quickly broken.

Have you ever broken a pencil with your own bare hands? Just snapped it in half, like the Incredible Hulk? Go ahead, try it. (With permission, of course. Don't go breaking pencils that don't belong to you or if your parents don't want you to!)

Now, take three pencils and hold them together in your hands and try to snap all three of them! (Just use your imagination if you don't have three pencils.) Not so easy, is it? Why?

Because those pencils are supporting each other. They give strength to each other. These three pencils, alone, would break beneath your awesome power. But together, they are able to withstand the force against them.

That's what good friends look like. That's what our key verse means. When powerful temptations or sadness or terrible days happen, good friends help support each other.

• Why are you and your friends like pencils?

• Why would you want your friendships to be like a "cord of three strands" . . . or a bundle of three pencils?

Part Four:
"FRIENDSHIP" IN THE STORY

Thinking about the story, do you think that Daniel, Shadrach, Meshach, and Abednego might have known about our key verse? It was written before they were born, and it would have been in the scriptures they read, so they probably did!

They certainly acted like they knew it. Look at their actions as they were thrown into the most horrible of situations. They were taken away from their family and their homes to a far away land, they were forced to work for the people who took them away, and then they were being told to eat food that, according to their traditions and laws, was bad for them.

They could have easily just gone along with it. But they knew that would be wrong for them to do. But to not eat that food, even though they knew they should not, would not be an easy thing to do.

They did it together, though. And just like the verse says, "a cord of three strands is not easily broken." (Also, they had four!)

Years later, as adults, their friendship remained strong. When Daniel needed help and encouragement, he was able to call on them to pray with him and support him. And in the next two parts of Shadrach, Meshach, and Abednego's story, we will see how those three strands help each other stand again!

• What are some things we can learn about friendship from this story of Daniel, Shadrach, Meshach, and Abednego?

• What kind of things can you and your friends do to be like the friends in the story?

Part Five:
"FRIENDSHIP" IN OUR LIVES

Do you have friends like Daniel, Shadrach, Meshach, and Abednego? Are you a friend like Daniel, Shadrach, Meshach, and Abednego? Are your friendships like the "cord of three strands"? (Or maybe the bundle of three pencils?)

When you are with your friends, do you encourage each other to make good choices? When you are with a group that is telling mean jokes about someone, would you and your friends try to put a stop to it? Or would you join in? When watching TV or using the computer and something comes on you know you shouldn't watch, would you and your friends encourage each other to turn it off? Or would you all stay silent and just watch?

Being a good friend, like the friends in the story and the verse, sometimes means making hard choices or doing difficult things. Sometimes it means doing unpopular things. But it means doing it together.

Friends are a gift from God. God has given us friends to help us learn about him and to encourage each other to grow more like Jesus.

- What are some ways you can encourage your friends?
- What can you do to make your friendships like a "cord of three strands"?

ACTION ACTIVITY: FRIENDSHIP

Think of a good friend (or more than one, if you can). Write a note to them telling them some of the things you appreciate about them and thanking them for their friendship. Send it to them. If you are doing this with your family or a group, tell everyone who you chose to write a note to and why.

- How do you think your friend will feel when they get your note?

THE IDOL

Hero: Shadrach, Meshach, & Abednego
　　　(part 2 of 3)
Hero Trait: Faithfulness
Key Verse: I Samuel 12:24
Story From: Daniel 3:1-18

OVER THE YEARS, SHADRACH, MESHACH, AND ABEDNEGO WERE APPOINTED TO HIGH PLACES IN THE BABYLONIAN GOVERNMENT.

THEIR FRIENDSHIP REMAINED STRONG, AND THEY WERE IN FAVOR WITH THE KING OF BABYLON.

BUT WHILE THEY FOLLOWED GOD, THE KING OF BABYLON DID NOT.

HE ORDERED THAT AN ENORMOUS STATUE BE BUILT OUTSIDE THE CITY.

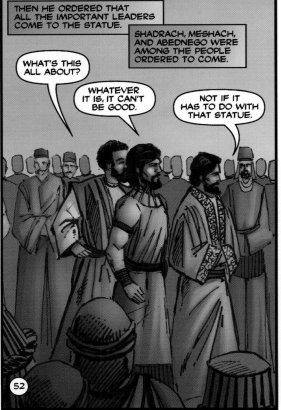

THEN HE ORDERED THAT ALL THE IMPORTANT LEADERS COME TO THE STATUE.

SHADRACH, MESHACH, AND ABEDNEGO WERE AMONG THE PEOPLE ORDERED TO COME.

WHAT'S THIS ALL ABOUT?

WHATEVER IT IS, IT CAN'T BE GOOD.

NOT IF IT HAS TO DO WITH THAT STATUE.

THEN A HERALD MADE AN ANNOUNCEMENT:

LISTEN, EVERYONE!

WHEN YOU HEAR THE SOUND OF INSTRUMENTS PLAYING, YOU ARE TO BOW DOWN!!!

FALL TO YOUR KNEES AND WORSHIP THIS STATUE!

IF YOU DON'T, YOU WILL BE THROWN INTO A BLAZING FURNACE!!!

Doot-Doo-
Doo-Dee-
Doo-Dee-
Dooo

AND WHEN THE INSTRUMENTS PLAYED...

...EVERYONE BOWED, PROVING THEY WERE FAITHFUL TO KING NEBUCHADNEZZAR AND HIS GODS.

...MOST EVERYONE...

ONCE AGAIN, TOLD TO DO SOMETHING WE CAN'T DO.

A BIT MORE DANGEROUS THIS TIME.

WE WORSHIP ONLY THE TRUE GOD. WE MUST BE FAITHFUL TO HIM.

53

WORD ABOUT THE THREE MEN WAS BROUGHT TO THE KING.

THIS IS AN OUTRAGE!!!

WHAT DID YOU SEE?

GREAT KING NEBUCHADNEZZAR, THOSE THREE HEBREW MEN YOU PUT IN SUCH HIGH POSITIONS DO NOT RESPECT YOU.

THEY WILL NOT BOW TO YOUR STATUE.

THEY SAID SOMETHING ABOUT BEING FAITHFUL TO THEIR GOD.

BRING THEM TO ME!!!

LATER, SHADRACH, MESHACH, AND ABEDNEGO WERE BROUGHT BEFORE THE KING.

I HAVE HEARD A DISTURBING RUMOR.

THEY SAY THAT YOU THREE WILL NOT BOW TO MY STATUE!

AND I HAVE SAID THAT ANYONE WHO DOES NOT BOW WILL BE THROWN INTO A FIERY FURNACE.

BUT YOU THREE HAVE DONE GOOD WORK FOR ME AND FOR BABYLON.

SO I OFFER YOU A SECOND CHANCE.

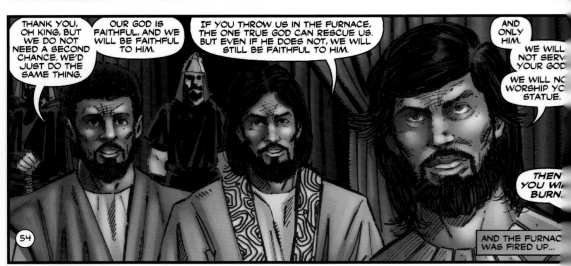

THANK YOU, OH KING, BUT WE DO NOT NEED A SECOND CHANCE. WE'D JUST DO THE SAME THING.

OUR GOD IS FAITHFUL, AND WE WILL BE FAITHFUL TO HIM.

IF YOU THROW US IN THE FURNACE, THE ONE TRUE GOD CAN RESCUE US. BUT EVEN IF HE DOES NOT, WE WILL STILL BE FAITHFUL TO HIM.

AND ONLY HIM.

WE WILL NOT SERV YOUR GOD

WE WILL NO WORSHIP YO STATUE.

THEN YOU WI BURN.

AND THE FURNAC WAS FIRED UP...

Part Two:
"FAITHFULNESS"

FAITHFULNESS: *Choosing to be loyal, dependable, and trustworthy.*

In chapter 1 of Shadrach, Meshach, and Abednego's story, we saw these friends stand together in an uncomfortable situation. In this chapter, they stood together in a situation that wasn't just uncomfortable, it was deadly! But, even with their lives on the line, they were faithful to God and to each other.

What does "faithfulness" mean? It means you choose to be committed to something or someone. A faithful sports fan cheers for his favorite team. A faithful friend helps his or her friends. Dogs are considered faithful pets, because they are committed to their owners.

Being faithful means being loyal and dependable. It means being honest and trustworthy. The best example of "faithfulness" is God. He is faithful to us. He loves us no matter what. He cares for us and listens to us and teaches us. He is more dependable and trustworthy than any person in the entire universe.

We are not perfect like God, but we can be faithful to him like he is to us. We do this by being loyal to him, following his commands, studying the Bible, talking about him to other people, and choosing to serve him.

- What are some ways God is faithful to us?

- How can we be faithful to our friends? To God?

Part Three:
"FAITHFULNESS" IN THE BIBLE

I Samuel 12:24 But be sure to fear the Lord and serve him faithfully with all your heart; consider what great things he has done for you.

This is a good verse because it reminds us of two things: first, it reminds us to be faithful to God; second, it reminds us about how God has been faithful to us.

When you think of a faithful pet, why is that pet faithful? Because its owners took care of it. Its owner was faithful.

Why are children faithful to their parents? Because their parents took care of them. Their parents were faithful.

And why should we be faithful to God? Because God has been, always is, and forever will be faithful to us!

- When you "consider the great things he has done for you," what are some things that God has done for you that you can remember?

- Can you think of someone who "serves the Lord faithfully"? What are some things that person does?

ACTION ACTIVITY: FAITHFULNESS

Find a chair that gets used often. (If you are doing this with a group or your family, put it in the middle of the room where you can all see it.) Before looking at the questions, take turns sitting in the chair.

- When you sat in the chair, did you worry if it would hold you or not? Why?

- What are other things in your life that are "faithful" -- in other words, things that you rely on because they are always steady and stable when you need them?

Part Four:

"FAITHFULNESS" IN THE STORY

In chapter 1 of their story, we learned about how these friends relied on each other when they were young. Maybe that was even the first time they realized how much they could rely on God! Over the years, their relationship with each other and with God grew.

Until the events from today's chapter. Now, they faced a life and death situation. They were told to bow down and worship someone other than God or they would be killed.

They chose to stand. They chose not to bow down.

It probably was not easy for them. It was probably very scary. But they stood together. They were faithful to each other. They were faithful to God. And they trusted that he would be faithful to them!

Just like the verse said, they "served God faithfully", remembering the "great things he had done for them"!

• How did Shadrach, Meshach, and Abednego show faithfulness to each other? How did they show faithfulness to God?

• What made it easier for them to stand and not bow down to the statue?

Part Five:
"FAITHFULNESS" IN OUR LIVES

You probably don't have anyone forcing you to bow down to an idol, but there are always things in our lives that can distract us from God and make us less faithful.

For example, we show our faithfulness in how we spend our time. Playing video games or spending time online are not always bad, but what if you spend all your time doing those things instead of spending time with friends, or with family, or with God?

"Faithfulness" is a hard quality to have. It takes work. There are many things around us that can distract us from being faithful, especially being faithful to God. If other people are making fun of someone, it can be easy to join in. It feels good to say something and make people laugh! But, being faithful means doing the things God wants us to do, and sometimes that means taking a stand, like Shadrach, Meshach, and Abednego. Instead of making fun of that person, maybe it means asking people to stop or trying to make that person feel better. This won't get you thrown into a fiery furnace, as we'll see in the next chapter of their story, but it may mean you get made fun of, too, which doesn't feel good.

But that's part of the "faithfulness circle." The faithfulness circle comes from our verse: we remember how God was faithful to us, we are faithful to God and that might mean bad things happen (like getting made fun of . . . or a fiery furnace), God is with us and takes care of us and is faithful to us, then we remember how God was faithful to us, we are faithful to God . . . and on and on it goes!

• What are some things that make it difficult to be faithful to other people? To God?

• What are some things we can do to show faithfulness to God?

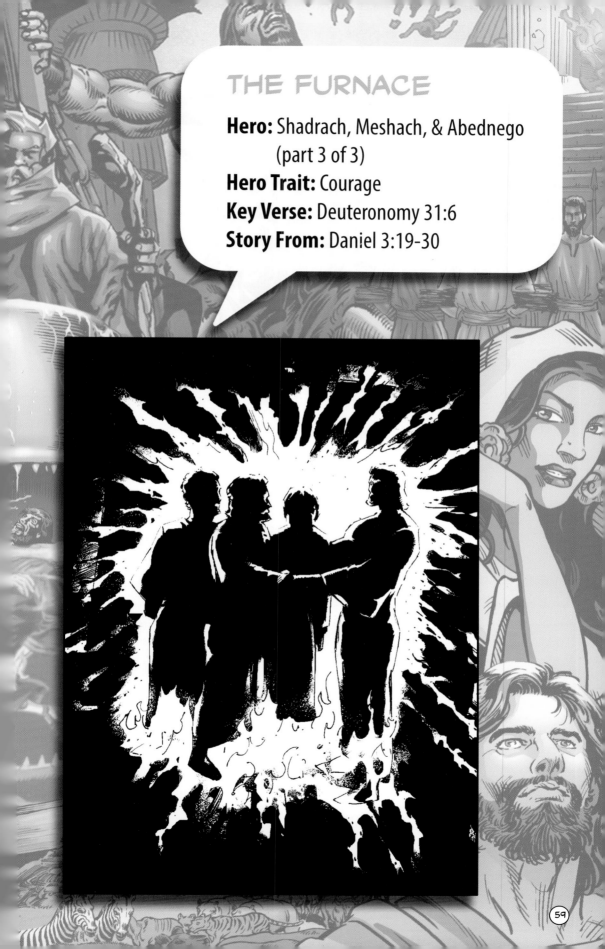

THE FURNACE

Hero: Shadrach, Meshach, & Abednego
(part 3 of 3)
Hero Trait: Courage
Key Verse: Deuteronomy 31:6
Story From: Daniel 3:19-30

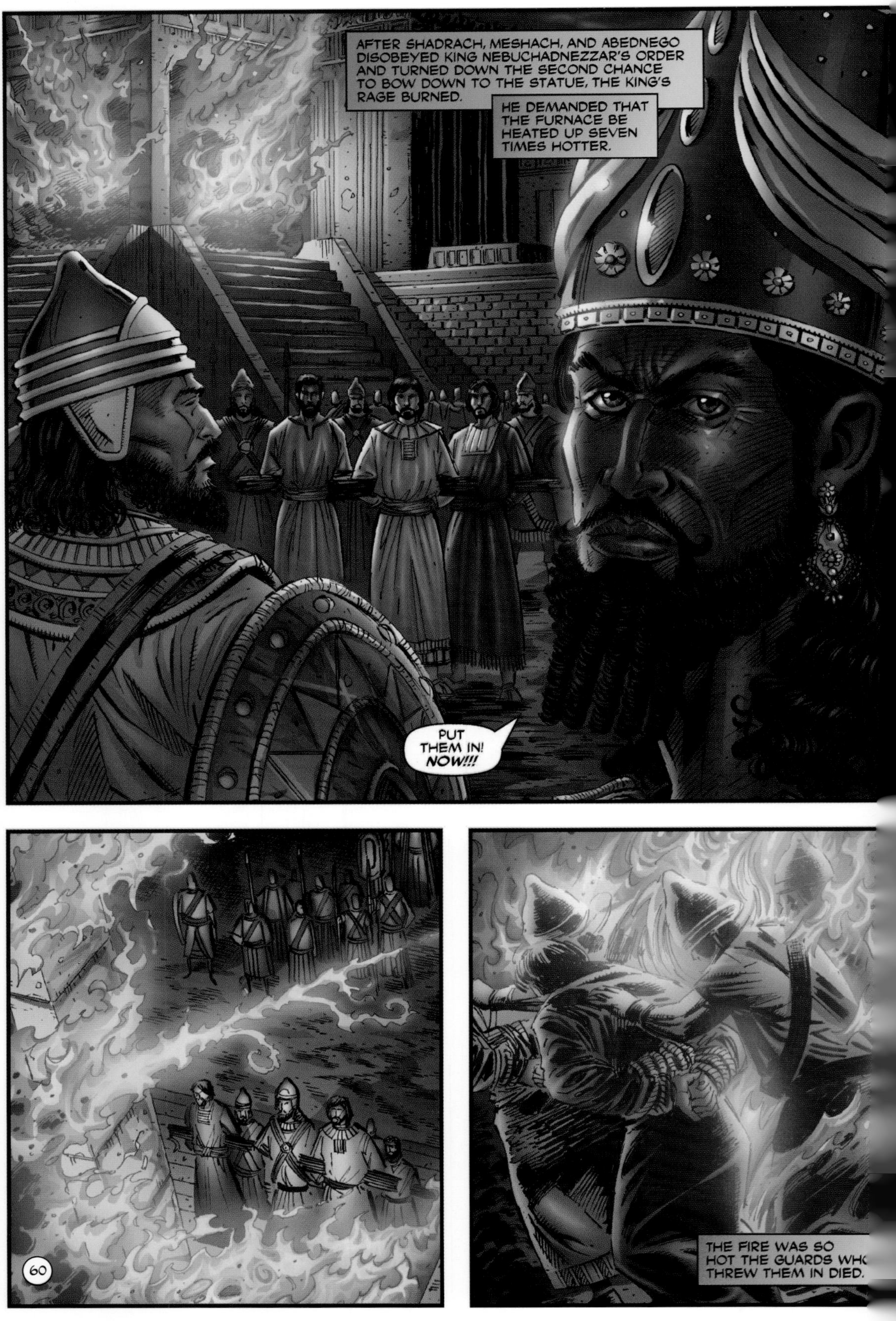
AFTER SHADRACH, MESHACH, AND ABEDNEGO DISOBEYED KING NEBUCHADNEZZAR'S ORDER AND TURNED DOWN THE SECOND CHANCE TO BOW DOWN TO THE STATUE, THE KING'S RAGE BURNED.
HE DEMANDED THAT THE FURNACE BE HEATED UP SEVEN TIMES HOTTER.
PUT THEM IN! *NOW!!!*
THE FIRE WAS SO HOT THE GUARDS WH THREW THEM IN DIED.

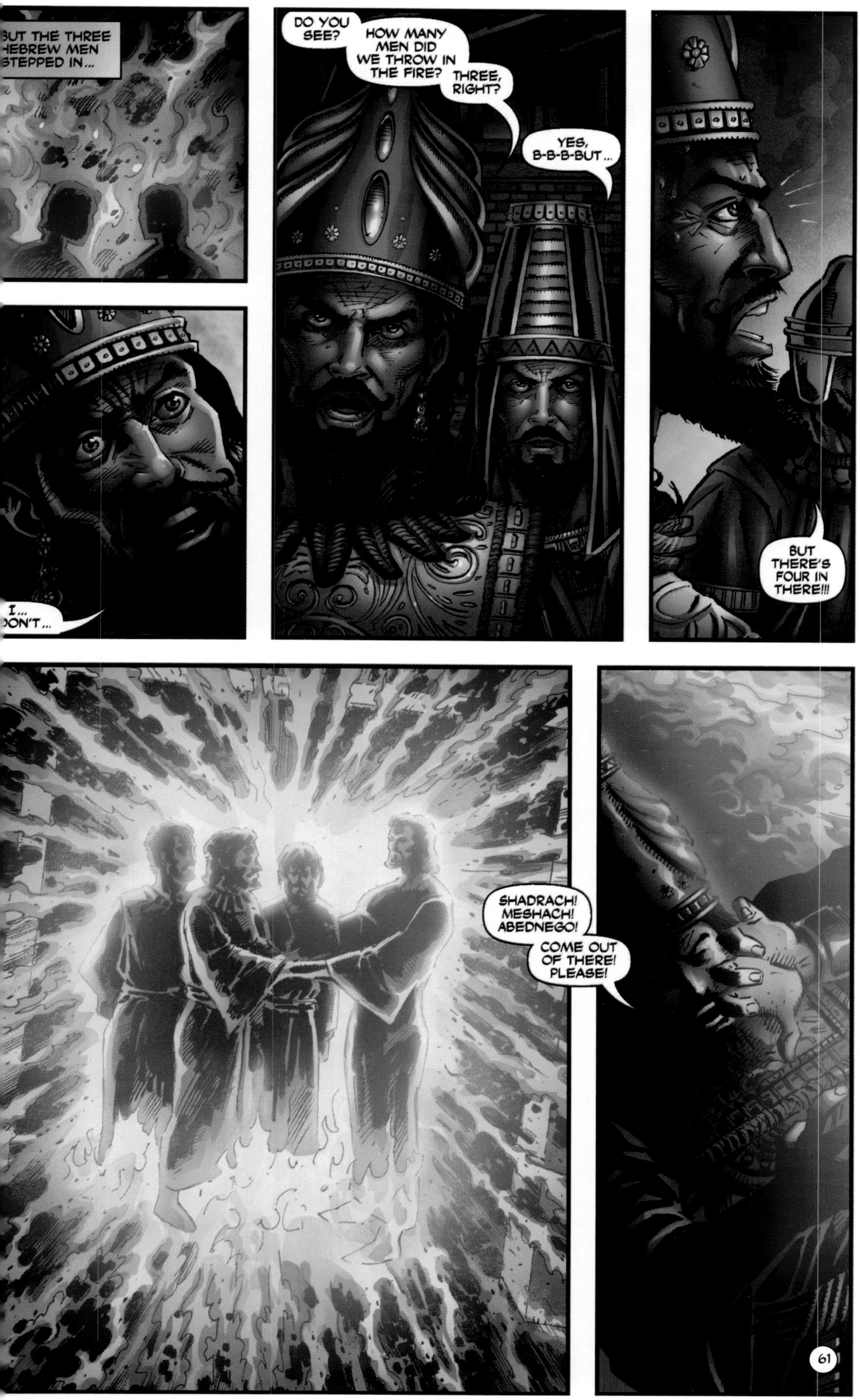
BUT THE THREE HEBREW MEN STEPPED IN...
I... DON'T...
DO YOU SEE?
HOW MANY MEN DID WE THROW IN THE FIRE?
THREE, RIGHT?
YES, B-B-B-BUT...
BUT THERE'S FOUR IN THERE!!!
SHADRACH! MESHACH! ABEDNEGO!
COME OUT OF THERE! PLEASE!

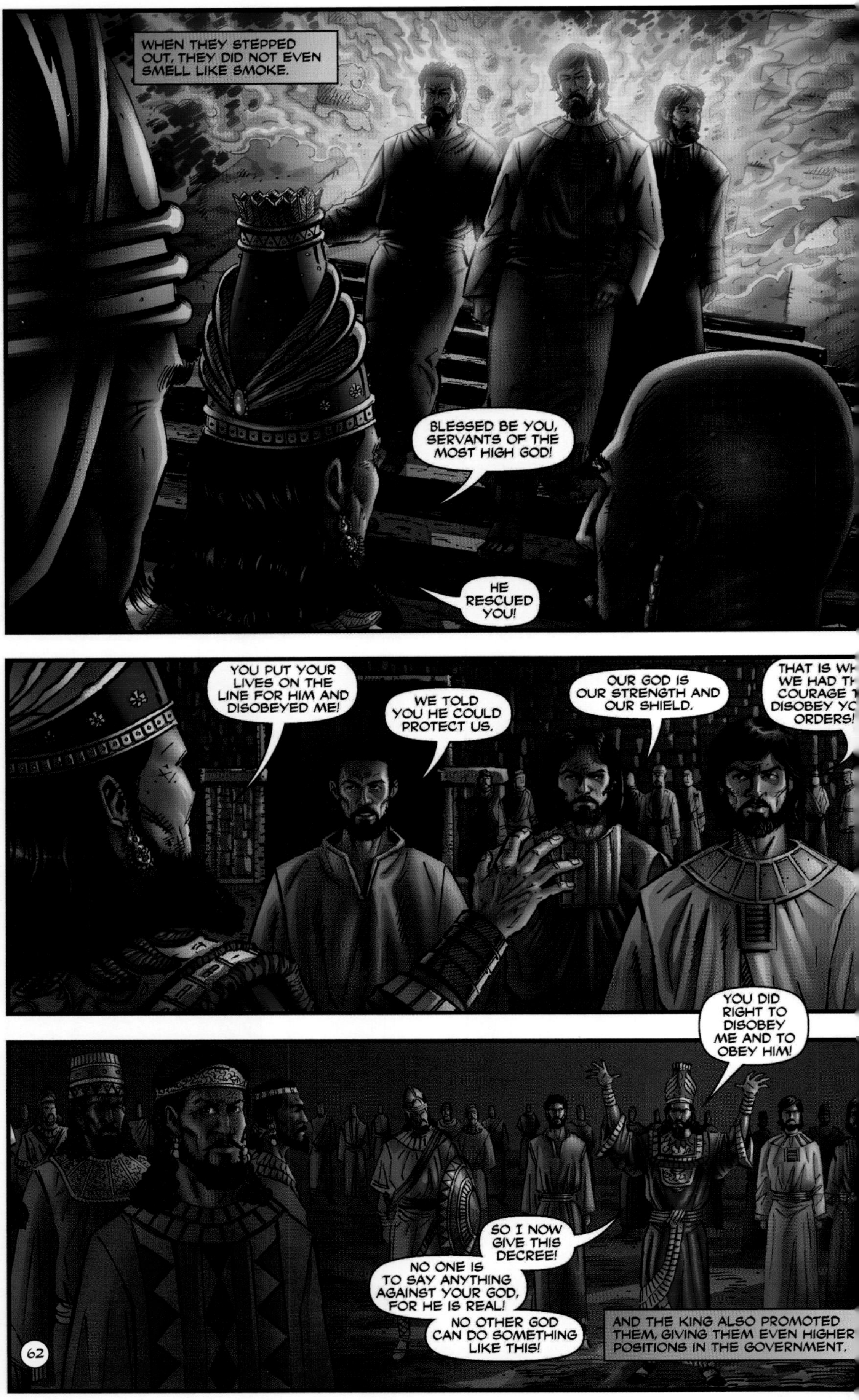
WHEN THEY STEPPED OUT, THEY DID NOT EVEN SMELL LIKE SMOKE.
BLESSED BE YOU, SERVANTS OF THE MOST HIGH GOD!
HE RESCUED YOU!
YOU PUT YOUR LIVES ON THE LINE FOR HIM AND DISOBEYED ME!
WE TOLD YOU HE COULD PROTECT US.
OUR GOD IS OUR STRENGTH AND OUR SHIELD.
THAT IS W WE HAD T COURAGE DISOBEY YO ORDERS!
YOU DID RIGHT TO DISOBEY ME AND TO OBEY HIM!
SO I NOW GIVE THIS DECREE!
NO ONE IS TO SAY ANYTHING AGAINST YOUR GOD, FOR HE IS REAL!
NO OTHER GOD CAN DO SOMETHING LIKE THIS!
AND THE KING ALSO PROMOTED THEM, GIVING THEM EVEN HIGHER POSITIONS IN THE GOVERNMENT.

Part Two:
"COURAGE"

COURAGE: *Facing difficult or scary situations without fear because you know God is with you.*

What is courage? And where does courage come from?

When you have courage, it means that you are able to face situations that might be dangerous or scary. Having courage means that you are confident that you can not just face that situation, but that you have the ability to overcome it . . . even if it seems like it is just too much to handle.

But courage for a Christian is different than just feeling like you can handle a tough situation. Christians' courage comes from confidence. They know that God is on their side and they know that God is in control. Suddenly, facing a tough situation doesn't seem so tough, because God is bigger than any situation you could face.

Like the situation Shadrach, Meshach, and Abednego faced.

- What is courage?
- Where does true courage come from?

Part Three:
"COURAGE" IN THE BIBLE

Deuteronomy 31:6 *Be strong and courageous. Do not be afraid or terrified because of them, for the Lord your God goes with you; he will never leave you nor forsake you.*

What an incredible promise and reminder this verse is!

Having courage doesn't mean foolishly jumping into dangerous situations, but it does mean that when scary or difficult situations come, you can be confident that God is right there with you.

Just because someone is a Christian, doesn't mean that bad things stop happening. We live in a world with people who choose to do hurtful things. We live in a world that has storms, earthquakes, and sickness.

But God is also here with us in this world. And in another verse of the Bible we are reminded that "…the one who is in you is greater than the one who is in the world." (1 John 4:4b)

- How does a verse like this give a Christian more reason to feel courage?

- Imagine how this verse might have encouraged Shadrach, Meshach, and Abednego. What could their conversation have been like as they were waiting to be put in the furnace?

ACTION ACTIVITY: COURAGE

For this you need some cotton balls and some paper (with a target drawn on it) or a bowl. Starting close to the target or bowl, take turns throwing a cotton ball at the target. After every throw, take a step backward. (This could be a game to see who can get the most cotton balls in. After three misses, you're out!) Keep moving backward and trying to hit the target.

- Why did it get more difficult to hit the target? When was it easiest?

- Like throwing the cotton balls, the closer we are to God, the easier it is to have courage. What are some ways to get closer to God?

Part Four:
"COURAGE" IN THE STORY

The words spoken by Shadrach, Meshach, and Abednego when they faced the king about disobeying his decree are famous words. They are bold words. They are courageous words.

Shadrach, Meshach, and Abednego were about to be punished. And the punishment was death! The king decided to be nice and did something he didn't have to do. He could have just thrown them into the furnace and forgotten about them! Instead, he gave them a second chance. A second chance to obey him . . . and disobey God.

Their answer: "O Nebuchadnezzar, we do not need to defend ourselves before you in this matter. If we are thrown into the blazing furnace, the God we serve is able to save us from it, and he will rescue us from your hand, O king. But even if he does not, we want you to know, O king, that we will not serve your gods or worship the image of gold you have set up." (Daniel 3:16b-18)

In other words: we know that God can protect us from your death trap, but even if he doesn't, we're still going to do the right thing!

They had courage. Courage to do what was right. Courage to stand in front of the king of the land and tell him they served only God. Courage, because they knew God was with them.

- What do you think gave them the courage they had?

- How does the trait of "faithfulness" from chapter 2 of Shadrach, Meshach, and Abednego's story help someone have courage?

Part Five:
"COURAGE" IN OUR LIVES

What about you? Are there any things that you need courage to face?

Courage can be needed in little things and in big things. Sometimes, courage is needed when you have to tell a parent or a teacher or a friend the truth. When you are about to get into trouble for doing something, you might be tempted to lie because it is easier. But the truth, even though sometimes harder to tell, is always the best answer . . . and we need courage to say it.

Sometimes courage is needed to speak up to a friend and confront them about something they are doing that is wrong.

Sometimes, courage is needed to try something new, like trying out for a team or a music group. Or going to a new school.

Sometimes courage is needed when things are completely out of your control, like if your parents are getting a divorce or if your family is moving.

But when you need courage, remember this story and this verse.

- What are some things you need courage for?

- How can our verse -- "Be strong and courageous... for it is the Lord your God who goes with you. He will not leave you or forsake you." -- help you to be courageous?

THE BABY
AND THE BARN

Hero: Mary & Joseph
Hero Trait: Contentment
Key Verse: Hebrews 13:5
Story From: Luke 2:4-7

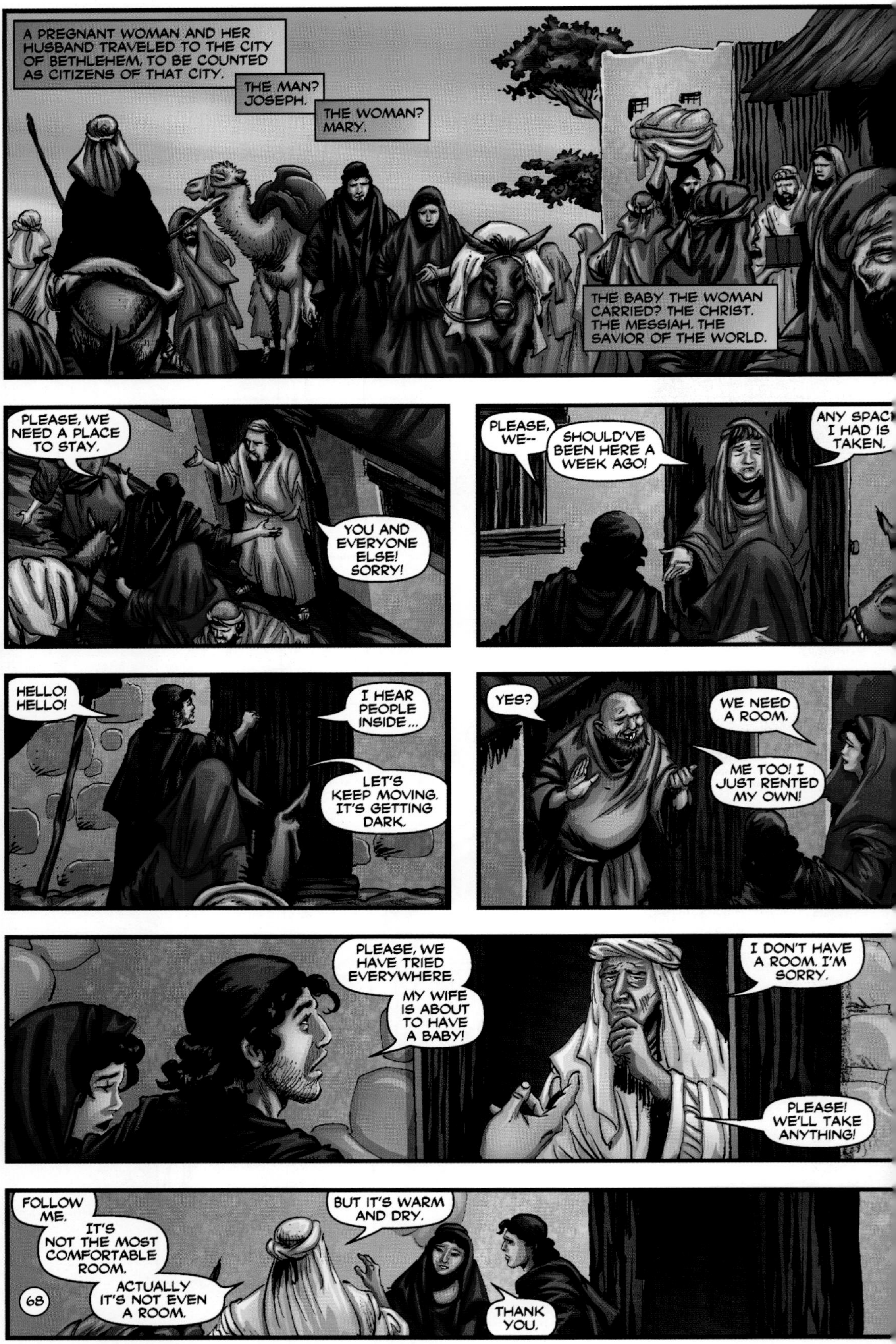
A PREGNANT WOMAN AND HER HUSBAND TRAVELED TO THE CITY OF BETHLEHEM, TO BE COUNTED AS CITIZENS OF THAT CITY.
THE MAN? JOSEPH.
THE WOMAN? MARY.
THE BABY THE WOMAN CARRIED? THE CHRIST. THE MESSIAH. THE SAVIOR OF THE WORLD.
PLEASE, WE NEED A PLACE TO STAY.
YOU AND EVERYONE ELSE! SORRY!
PLEASE, WE--
SHOULD'VE BEEN HERE A WEEK AGO!
ANY SPAC I HAD IS TAKEN.
HELLO! HELLO!
I HEAR PEOPLE INSIDE...
LET'S KEEP MOVING. IT'S GETTING DARK.
YES?
WE NEED A ROOM.
ME TOO! I JUST RENTED MY OWN!
PLEASE, WE HAVE TRIED EVERYWHERE.
MY WIFE IS ABOUT TO HAVE A BABY!
I DON'T HAVE A ROOM. I'M SORRY.
PLEASE! WE'LL TAKE ANYTHING!
FOLLOW ME.
IT'S NOT THE MOST COMFORTABLE ROOM.
ACTUALLY IT'S NOT EVEN A ROOM.
BUT IT'S WARM AND DRY.
THANK YOU.

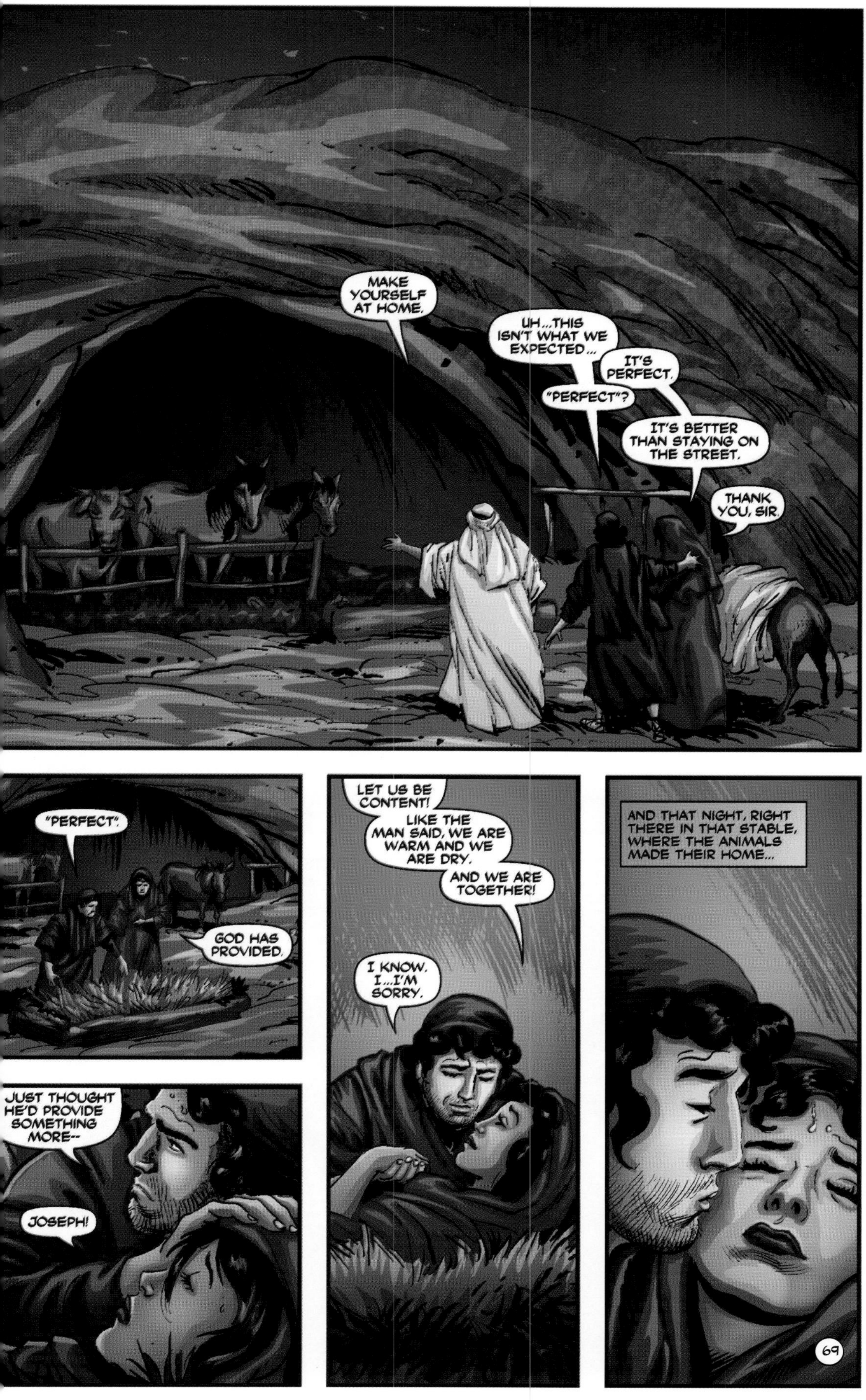
MAKE YOURSELF AT HOME.
UH...THIS ISN'T WHAT WE EXPECTED...
IT'S PERFECT.
"PERFECT"?
IT'S BETTER THAN STAYING ON THE STREET.
THANK YOU, SIR.
"PERFECT".
GOD HAS PROVIDED.
JUST THOUGHT HE'D PROVIDE SOMETHING MORE--
JOSEPH!
LET US BE CONTENT!
LIKE THE MAN SAID, WE ARE WARM AND WE ARE DRY.
AND WE ARE TOGETHER!
I KNOW. I...I'M SORRY.
AND THAT NIGHT, RIGHT THERE IN THAT STABLE, WHERE THE ANIMALS MADE THEIR HOME...

...THE CHILD WAS BORN!

THE ONE WHO WOULD SHOW THE WORLD GOD'S LOVE IN A WAY NO ONE ELSE COULD.

THE ONE WHO WOULD SAVE THE WORLD FROM ITS SIN.

EXCUSE US!

YOU MAY NOT BELIEVE THIS, BUT--

--ANGELS TOLD US THERE WAS A BABY BORN HERE!

IS THIS THE BABY THEY WERE TELLIN' US ABOUT?

WHAT AN UNLIKELY PLACE FOR A BABY THAT ANGELS ANNOUNCED!

PERHAPS, PERHAPS NOT.

AND THERE, IN THAT PLACE, MARY AND JOSEPH DID NOT CARE THAT THEIR BEDS WERE HAY.

THAT THEY SHARED IT WITH ANIMALS.

FOR THERE, IN THAT HUMBLE PLACE, THE CHILD THAT WOULD CHANGE HISTORY HAD BEEN BORN.

Part Two:
"CONTENTMENT"

CONTENTMENT: *Choosing to be happy with the things and circumstances God has given you.*

Have you ever felt like things weren't fair?

Have you ever complained because things weren't going your way?

If so, you have probably heard our word. Maybe a parent or a teacher or even a friend or sibling has said to you, "Be content."

What, exactly, does that mean? It means that when things aren't going your way or aren't fair, to still be happy with what God has given you. It is the opposite of being greedy.

When you are content, it means you may still work hard for the things you need, but it also means that you recognize and remember all the good things God has given you.

- What are some times when you do not feel content?
- When is it easy to feel content?

ACTION ACTIVITY: CONTENTMENT

Count your blessings. Trace your hand on a piece of paper. In each finger, write something you are thankful for. Share your list.

- How can "counting your blessings" or being thankful for what you have help you to feel content?

Part Three:
"CONTENTMENT" IN THE BIBLE

Hebrews 13:5 *Keep your lives free from the love of money and be content with what you have, because God has said, "Never will I leave you; never will I forsake you."*

When we think about things that make us feel discontented (the opposite of content), it often has to do with money. "If I could just buy this or buy that, I would be happy."

Our verse tells us to "be content with what you have." Does this mean that you should never give Grandma or Grandpa or Mom or Dad your Christmas list? Or never try to earn money to buy a new bike? No.

But this verse is a reminder to be content when we don't have the things we want, like the things from that Christmas list or that bike. When we don't have those things, we need to remember that we do have something far more valuable. God himself has said, "I will never leave you or forsake you."

Think about that. Money gets spent or lost. Bikes get rusty. Toys break. Treats get eaten. But God, who knows all that you need, will never leave you. God, who created all the things we use to make the paper and plastic things we want so much, loves you and will never desert you.

That's something to help you feel content.

- How does this verse help us remember to be content?
- When can it be wrong to want something? When is it not wrong?

Part Four:
"CONTENTMENT" IN THE STORY

Mary was having a baby. This was an important baby, yes, because the baby was Jesus. But all babies are important, and mothers want to have their babies in clean, safe places.

Not barns.

Mary could have complained. She could have said, "This isn't fair! I am having the most important baby ever born in the history of the world!" (And she'd be right about this baby being the most important baby in the history of the world!) "I should be given a better place! I should be in the most comfortable room! I should have the most skilled and trained people to help my baby come! This is not fair!"

Instead, she and Joseph were content. God had given them a dry place. God had given them a warm place. (All those animals were like natural heaters!) God had given them a place that they never expected. It wasn't the most expensive or comfortable place, but God provided it for them.

We all know the Christmas story. We know that Jesus was born in this situation. But next time you hear or read the Christmas story, think about how Mary and Joseph were content with what God gave them.

- How would you feel if you were Mary or Joseph and had to stay in a place like that?

- What do you think helped them feel content in that situation?

Part Five:

"CONTENTMENT" IN OUR LIVES

It is easy to feel discontent sometimes. You may see friends who have the latest gadgets, or you may see commercials about some cool toys or shoes, or you may walk through a store and see something you want really badly.

But discontentment doesn't only apply to money and things. It can also be about situations. Maybe you don't like the house you live in, or you have to share a room with a brother or sister and don't want to. Maybe you don't like your school or your teacher. Maybe you are going through a tough family change.

Being content does not mean you have to like everything that happens. It does not mean you shouldn't try to change things that are bad. But it does mean when bad things are going on or when you don't have the things you want, you still remember that God is with you and God loves you. It means you try to look for the good things in your life that God has given you. Sometimes, it even means looking at some of the bad things that are happening and looking for how those might actually be good things.

• When something bad is happening, what are some ways you can try to be more content?

• Can you think of a bad thing that has happened that had some good come out of it? What was it?

THE LONG, LONG WAIT

Hero: Anna
Hero Trait: Hope
Key Verse: Jeremiah 29:11
Story From: Luke 2:36-38

ANNA'S DAY STARTED AS ANY OTHER DAY WOULD.

LIKE EVERY DAY, ANNA WENT TO THE TEMPLE TO PRAY.

SHE WAS A PROPHETESS: A WOMAN GOD GAVE SPECIAL KNOWLEDGE TO.

MANY YEARS AGO, HER HUSBAND HAD DIED AND SINCE THAT TIME SHE DEDICATED HER LIFE TO SERVING GOD.

SHE LIVED IN JERUSALEM, AND SPENT ALL HER TIME AT THE TEMPLE.

JERUSALEM AND THE COUNTRY OF ISRAEL WERE CONTROLLED BY THE ROMANS.

THE ROMANS WERE A STRONGER NATION WITH A POWERFUL ARMY. THE JEWS COULD NOT FIGHT THEM.

FOR YEARS, THE PEOPLE OF ISRAEL WAITED FOR SOMEONE TO DELIVER THEM.

ANNA, TOO, WAITED FOR THIS DELIVERER. THIS MESSIAH.

FOR YEARS, SINCE HER HUSBAND HAD DIED, SHE FASTED AND PRAYED IN THE TEMPLE.

PATIENTLY,
SHE WAITED.

PERSISTENTLY,
SHE PRAYED.

ANNA!

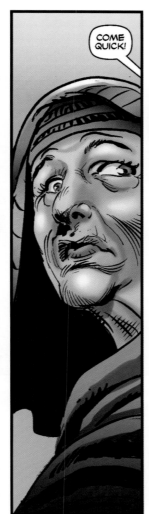

COME
QUICK!

COME! LOOK!
LOOK HERE!

WHAT?

BUT ON THAT ONE DAY,
A DAY LIKE ANY OTHER,
EVERYTHING CHANGED.

WHAT IS IT,
SIMEON?

SIMEON,
THIS BABY!

GOD SAID YOU
WOULD SEE
THE MESSIAH!

77

HOW MANY YEARS HAD SHE DEDICATED TO GOD, EVEN THOUGH SHE LOST EVERYTHING?

IT'S HIM!

HOW MANY YEARS HAD SHE PRAYED THAT SHE WOULD SEE THE DELIVERER?

HOW MANY YEARS HAD SHE WAITED FOR THIS MOMENT?

YOU TOLD EVERYONE YOU WOULD SEE HIM, SIMEON!

AND NOW I HAVE!

PEOPLE MUST KNOW!

LISTEN! LOOK! THE MESSIAH!

SOME OF US HAD GIVEN UP WAITING!

BUT HE IS HERE! NOW!

THE MESSIAH IS HERE!

GOD GAVE US HIS PROMISE!

AND GOD HAS FULFILLED IT!

Part Two:
"HOPE"

HOPE: *Expecting the best, even in a bad situation.*

Some people say that hope is "wishing for the best." But that's not the hope we are talking about here. That's not real hope. "Wishing" for something to happen just means wanting it to happen, and wanting something to happen never makes it happen.

But if your hope is in God, hope is something more special than that. Something more powerful.

Hope, when it comes from God, is not "wishing." Hope, when it comes from God, is "expecting"!

Hope, when it comes from God, means that even when things are bad, you know that God has good things planned for you!

So hope is not just "wishing for the best to happen." No, hope is "knowing the best WILL happen," because we know God.

- Why is it important to have hope in bad situations?
- How is "hoping" different than "wishing"?

ACTION ACTIVITY: HOPE

An acrostic is when you take the letters of one word and come up with words that start with those letters. Using the word HOPE, make an acrostic. Think of words that describe hope -- words that are about hope, that remind you of hope, or that can help you to have hope. (It's such a short word, see how many times you can do it with new words for the letters in HOPE!)

- Why did you use the words you used to describe hope?

Part Three:
"HOPE"
IN THE BIBLE

Jeremiah 29:11 *"For I know the plans I have for you," declares the Lord, "plans to prosper you and not to harm you, plans to give you hope and a future."*

This verse comes from a time in Israel's history when the people of Israel felt like they had no future. When they felt like they had no hope.

There was a long part of Israel's history when they were ruled by other countries. And if the country that controlled Israel was conquered by another country, Israel would just be under that new country's power.

But the prophet Jeremiah gave the people of Israel a message from God. "God has a plan," Jeremiah said, "and it may feel like we have no future, but guess what? God is a part of our future, so we can have hope!" Those are not his exact words -- he wrote a whole book about that message from God -- but that is the main idea.

And so this verse is a reminder to us, now, that God has a plan. When things feel horrible, God has a plan. God knows our future, God loves us very much, and we can have hope because of that!

• What are some other verses (from this book or that you already know) that can be a reminder for us to have hope?

• When things are bad, how does remembering that God has a plan for our future help us to have hope?

IN THE STORY

If anyone could give us an example of "hope," it's Anna.

Anna was what we call a "prophetess." God gave her special understanding of scripture. She listened to God. She listened to God, she prayed and fasted, and she knew things that God showed her. Because the Bible calls her a "prophetess" we can know that she told people about God.

Her husband died after they were married for only a short time. After he died, she spent almost all of her time worshipping and praying in the temple. She did this for many, many years. This was at a time when the people of Israel were not in control of their own country! The Romans ruled Israel, and the Romans did things that the people of Israel did not like.

A couple of hundred years before, the people of Israel were given a promise that a Messiah, or a savior, would come to rescue them. Some people grew tired of waiting. Some gave up. They had no hope in this bad situation.

But Anna did not give up hope. The Bible says she "never left the temple," which tells us that she was dedicated to serving God, even though she was waiting for the Messiah like everyone else. She waited with hope, knowing that God would fulfill the promise he gave.

And finally, when she was an old woman, she saw the baby Jesus, and she knew who he was. He was the Messiah she, and her people, had been waiting and hoping for.

- Do you think it was easy for Anna to have hope?

- How do you think Anna felt when she saw the baby Jesus?

Part Five:

"HOPE"
IN OUR LIVES

It is hard, sometimes, to have hope. Sometimes it feels like things that are happening are just too hard. Too scary. Too hurtful. Too sad. Sometimes, the things that happen to us or around us feel like a trap or feel like a cage.

Hope is the feeling we can have when we remember that if we feel like we are in a trap or in a cage, God is right there with us.

Hope is the feeling we can have when we do something really bad, but we know that God still loves us, no matter what. No matter how bad we feel about ourselves, God loves us!

Hope is the feeling we can have when we remember that God has an exciting plan for our life. Sometimes bad things happen because people make bad choices, and while sinful or hurtful things are not what God wants to happen, God can actually use those things to help us (like in our verse).

For people who follow God, hope is not just a warm and fuzzy feeling. Hope is more than just wishing for something good. Hope is knowing that God is good, that God loves us, and that God wants us to discover his awesome plan for our life!

- What are some things that can help us remember to have hope when we are in bad situations?

- If someone knows about God's love, how does that make hope different than if someone does not know about God's love?

THE BIG BATTLE

Hero: Jesus
Hero Trait: Wisdom
Key Verse: II Timothy 3:16
Story From: Matthew 4

AFTER HE WAS BAPTIZED, JESUS WAS LED INTO THE WILDERNESS BY THE HOLY SPIRIT.

HE PRAYED AND FASTED FOR FORTY DAYS...

...AND NIGHTS.

JESUS BECAME TIRED. WEAK.

HUNGRY.

AND IN THAT WEAK STATE, THE TEMPTER CAME TO HIM...

YOU ARE HUNGRY.

IF YOU REALLY ARE THE SON OF GOD, TURN THESE STONES INTO BREAD!

NO. IT IS WRITTEN: "MAN DOES NOT LIVE ON BREAD ALONE--

"--BUT ON EVERY WORD THAT COMES FROM THE MOUTH OF GOD."

84

THEN THE DEVIL TOOK JESUS TO JERUSALEM, TO THE HIGHEST PLACE OF THE TEMPLE.

IF YOU ARE THE SON OF GOD, PROVE IT!

JUMP!

ISN'T IT WRITTEN: "HE WILL COMMAND THE ANGELS WHO CARE FOR YOU, AND YOU WON'T HIT YOUR FOOT ON A SINGLE STONE"?

IT IS ALSO WRITTEN: "DO NOT PUT THE LORD TO THE TEST."

THE TEMPTER TOOK JESUS TO ANOTHER HIGH PLACE.

THIS TIME, A MOUNTAIN.

LOOK AT ALL THE KINGDOMS OF THE WORLD!

I'LL GIVE THEM OVER TO YOU IF YOU JUST BOW DOWN AND WORSHIP ME!

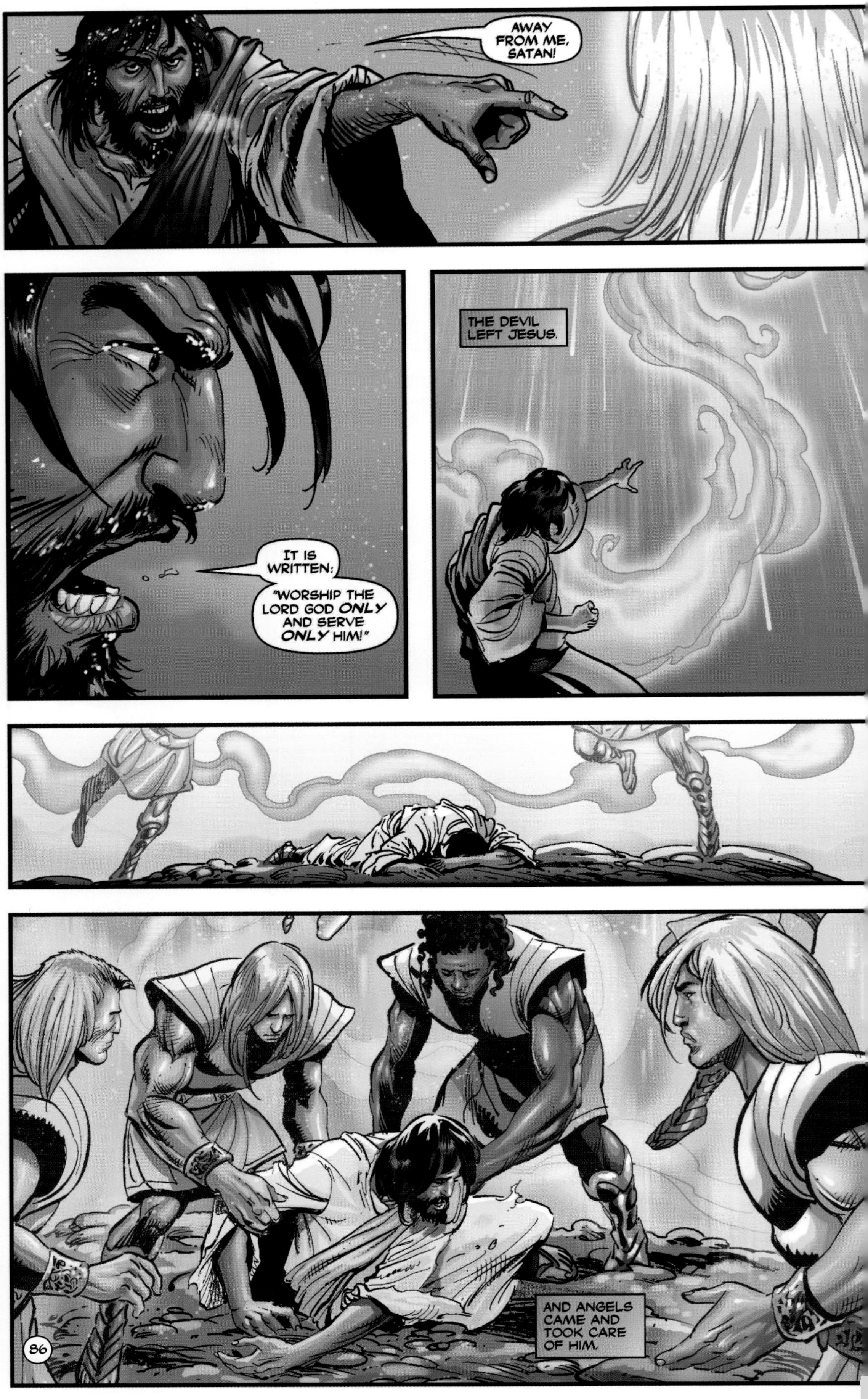
AWAY FROM ME, SATAN!
IT IS WRITTEN:
"WORSHIP THE LORD GOD ONLY AND SERVE ONLY HIM!"
THE DEVIL LEFT JESUS.
AND ANGELS CAME AND TOOK CARE OF HIM.

Part Two:
"WISDOM"

WISDOM: *Using knowledge to make choices that are good and right.*

It is easy to see why wisdom is a good character trait.

Wisdom means making good choices. Wisdom is not just knowing the right thing to do, but doing it. Wisdom is not just being smart, but using those smarts. Wisdom is knowing that you always have more to learn.

There are many, many verses in the Bible about the importance of wisdom. Maybe that is because when God gives us a gift, he expects us to use it. God gave you a brain. The brain is an amazing and wonderful part of the human body. Scientists still do not understand a lot about how it works. God gave it to you because he expects you to use it!

You might have heard someone say, "A wise man once said . . ." Then they finish that sentence with some good advice. What makes a person a "wise man"? It's not just knowledge, it is using knowledge to make good decisions.

• Who is the wisest person you know? What kind of things do they do that show you that they are wise?

• How could someone who is very smart not be very wise?

Part Three:
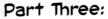
"WISDOM" IN THE BIBLE

II Timothy 3:16 *All scripture is God-breathed and is useful for teaching, rebuking, correcting, and training in righteousness...*

Where do you find wisdom? The first place to look is the Bible. The verses that we have chosen to put in this book come from the Bible and they were chosen because they are verses that will help you to make wise choices.

In the Bible, we find verses that help us to know the difference between right and wrong. In the Bible we find stories that show us both the right and wrong way to act. In the Bible, we find wise teachings that help us understand God and how much he loves us.

And when we learn the wisdom that the Bible teaches us, we can make wise choices. We can make wise choices about how we treat our brothers and sisters and friends. We can make wise choices about how we act in school and at home. We can make wise choices when our friends ask us to do something we know we should not do.

When we learn from the Bible, we learn how to make wise choices.

• Take a look back at some of the other verses in this book. Choose one. What kind of wise choice can that verse help you make?

• Look at the other Bible stories in this book. Choose one. What wisdom did you learn from that story?

Part Four:
"WISDOM"
IN THE STORY

In this story, we see Jesus in a battle against Satan. It was not a battle with weapons. No one punched or kicked anything. It was a spiritual battle.

Three times, Satan tried to convince Jesus to do something that would have been wrong for Jesus to do. He didn't use arrows or spears or bombs. Instead, those "temptations" were his attacks.

And three times, Jesus defended himself against those attacks. He did not use a sword or gun or nunchucks. What did he use? Verses from the Bible.

Whenever Satan tempted Jesus to do something, Jesus had a Bible verse ready to go that answered that temptation. This is a great example for us when we feel tempted to do something wrong or we need to make a difficult choice.

One way to do this is to read our Bible or do devotions like the ones found in this book. And when we have a difficult situation, we can always talk to someone who we know is wise and ask them to help us find answers in the Bible. Finally, we can memorize Bible verses, so, just like Jesus, we can have them right there in our mind, ready to be used.

- A couple of verses in the Bible compare the Bible to a sword. How is the Bible like a sword?

- Have you ever memorized any Bible verses? If not, what are some verses from this book you could learn? If you have, say one or two of them right now.

ACTION ACTIVITY: WISDOM

Look at the book of proverbs in your Bible. Use your birthday to find a Proverb -- use the month you were born in for the chapter and the day you were born on for the verse. (So October 16 would be Proverbs 10:16.) If there aren't enough verses in that chapter (like chapter 9, with only eighteen verses) flip it, so the day is the chapter and the month is the verse. Read it out loud.

- What wisdom does this verse teach?

Part Five:

Studying the Bible and learning Bible verses helps you learn wisdom, but don't forget that wisdom is not just having the information. Wisdom also means acting on that information. Just learning or knowing something does not do any good unless you use that knowledge.

That's why, when Jesus was being tempted, he didn't just say those Bible verses. He also refused to do what Satan was telling him to do.

Learning is the first step to being wise. Acting on what you have learned is the second step.

This is why memorizing Bible verses is important. It helps you remember the things you have learned about making wise choices, so when the time to act comes, it is easier to do the right thing.

Memorizing Bible verses takes time, but it is not hard. It really is as simple as saying the verses over and over again, just practicing them. Making the verse into a song can help you remember it. You can even make a game out of it and learn the verses together as a family! Not only can memorizing verses be fun to do, later on in your life you will be surprised that these verses come back to you just when you need them!

• What would happen if you never used any of the knowledge that you have learned?

• What are some ways you could make memorizing verses into a game?

THROUGH THE ROOF

Hero: The Four Friends
Hero Trait: Compassion
Key Verse: I John 3:18
Story From: Mark 2:1-12

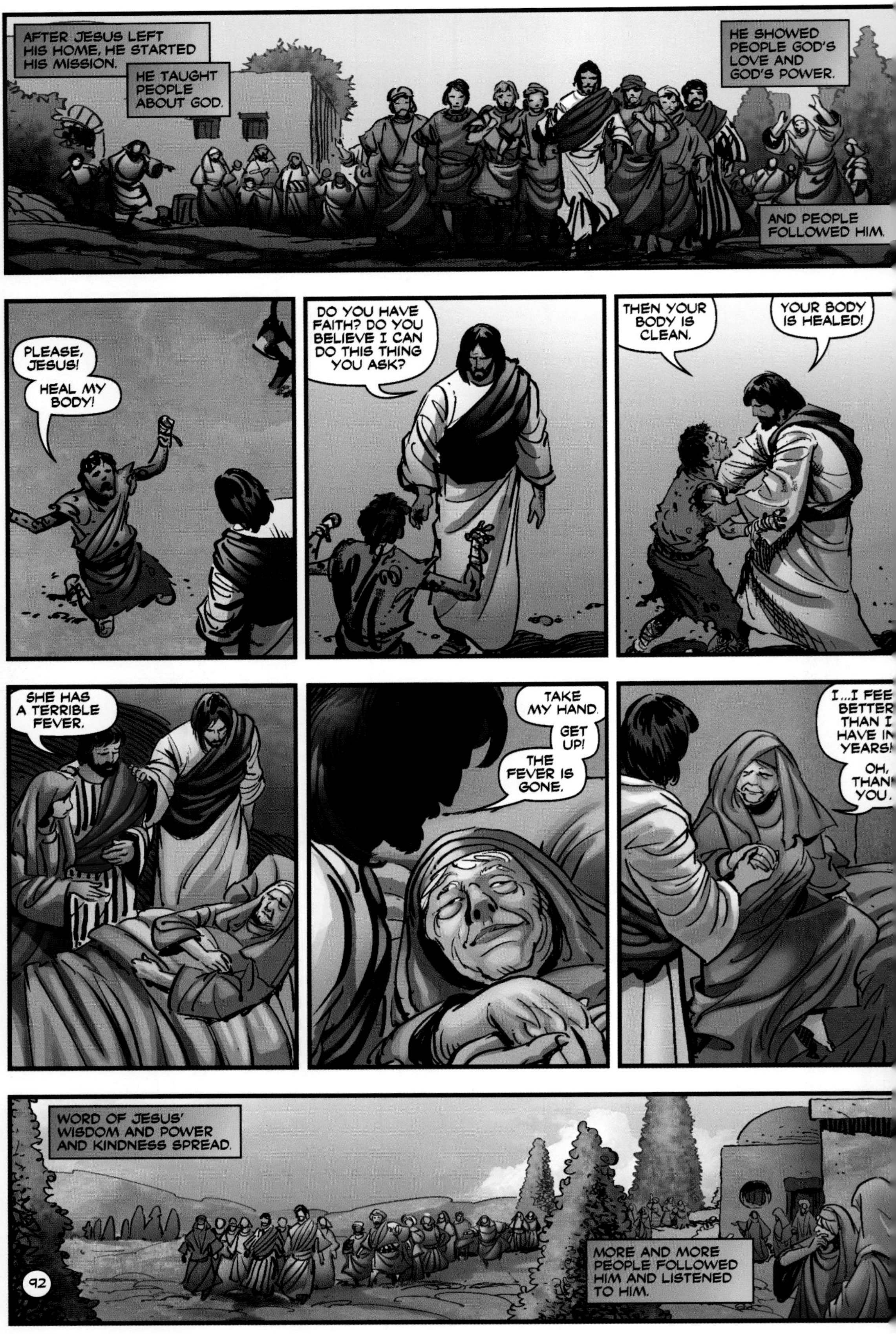
AFTER JESUS LEFT HIS HOME, HE STARTED HIS MISSION.
HE TAUGHT PEOPLE ABOUT GOD.
HE SHOWED PEOPLE GOD'S LOVE AND GOD'S POWER.
AND PEOPLE FOLLOWED HIM.
PLEASE, JESUS!
HEAL MY BODY!
DO YOU HAVE FAITH? DO YOU BELIEVE I CAN DO THIS THING YOU ASK?
THEN YOUR BODY IS CLEAN.
YOUR BODY IS HEALED!
SHE HAS A TERRIBLE FEVER.
TAKE MY HAND.
GET UP!
THE FEVER IS GONE.
WORD OF JESUS' WISDOM AND POWER AND KINDNESS SPREAD.
MORE AND MORE PEOPLE FOLLOWED HIM AND LISTENED TO HIM.

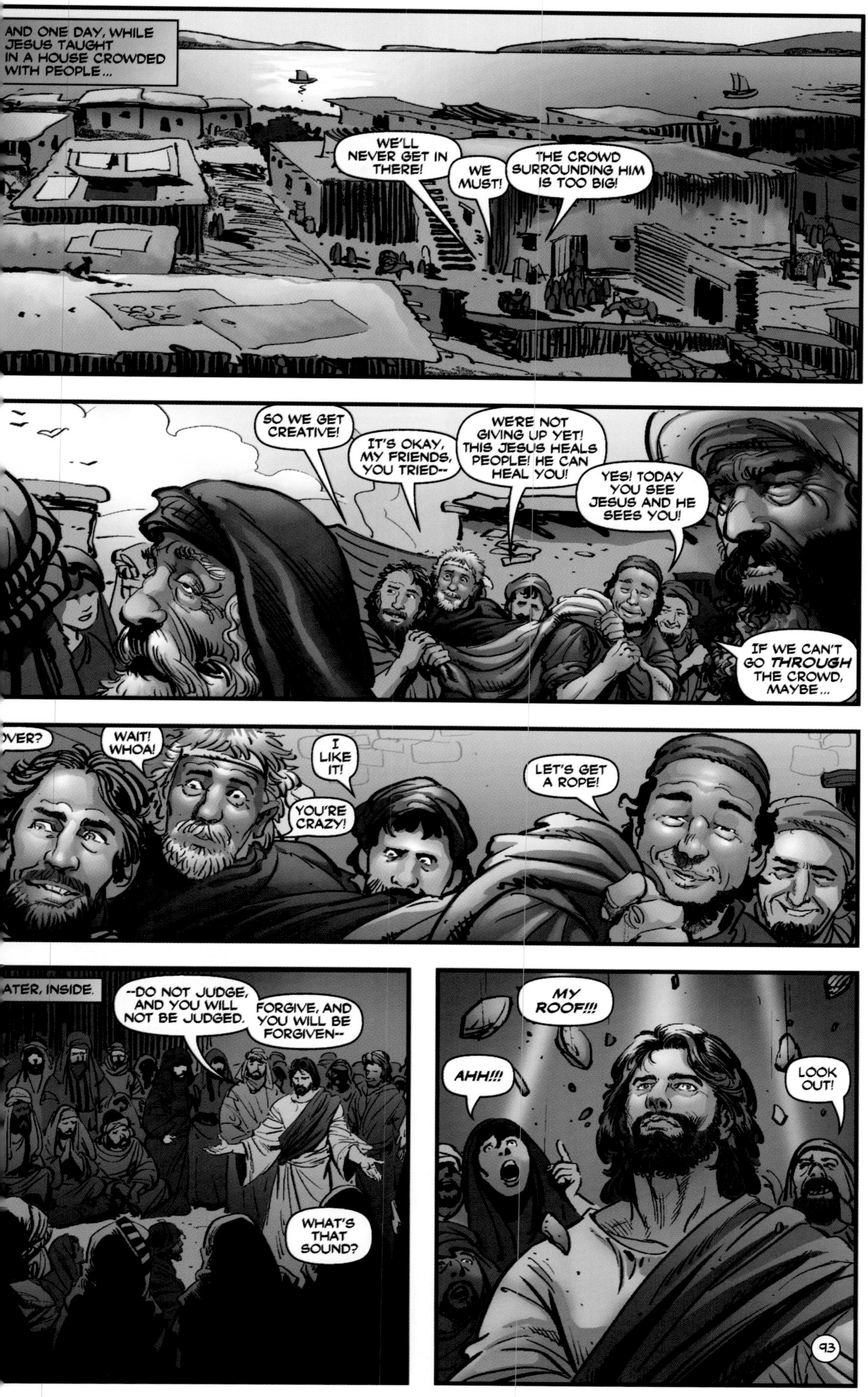
AND ONE DAY, WHILE JESUS TAUGHT IN A HOUSE CROWDED WITH PEOPLE...
WE'LL NEVER GET IN THERE!
WE MUST!
THE CROWD SURROUNDING HIM IS TOO BIG!
SO WE GET CREATIVE!
IT'S OKAY, MY FRIENDS, YOU TRIED--
WE'RE NOT GIVING UP YET! THIS JESUS HEALS PEOPLE! HE CAN HEAL YOU!
YES! TODAY YOU SEE JESUS AND HE SEES YOU!
IF WE CAN'T GO *THROUGH* THE CROWD, MAYBE...
OVER?
WAIT! WHOA!
I LIKE IT!
YOU'RE CRAZY!
LET'S GET A ROPE!
ATER, INSIDE.
--DO NOT JUDGE, AND YOU WILL NOT BE JUDGED.
FORGIVE, AND YOU WILL BE FORGIVEN--
WHAT'S THAT SOUND?
MY ROOF!!!
AHH!!!
LOOK OUT!

JESUS SAW THE MAN, LOWERED DOWN ON THE MAT HE USED FOR BEGGING.

HE SAW THE MAN'S FRIENDS. HE SAW THEIR FAITH AND THEIR COMPASSION.

AND HE HAD COMPASSION.

YOU HAVE FAITH IN ME.

YES, I DO. I DO.

THEN I FORGIVE YOUR SINS

OH, THANK YOU!

HOW DARE YOU SAY THAT? ONLY GOD CAN FORGIVE SINS!

WHAT'S EASIER TO SAY?

"YOUR SINS ARE FORGIVEN" OR "GET UP AND WALK"?

BUT, TO SHOW THAT I HAVE AUTHORITY TO FORGIVE SINS...

GET UP. TAKE YOUR MAT.

WHEN YOU LEAVE, LEAVE ON YOUR OWN TWO FEET.

I...I...I...

THANK YOU!

GUYS! GUYS! LOOK AT ME!

I'M WALKING!

NO! I'M RUNNIN'

Part Two:
"COMPASSION"

COMPASSION: *Showing concern for other people when they feel bad, are hurt, or need help.*

Compassion is showing concern for other people when they feel bad, are hurt, or need help. Someone who has compassion tries to understand how other people feel and then does what they can to help.

When you have compassion, you are showing love to other people. Having compassion is one of the most powerful ways to show you care for someone.

If you have ever been hurt and someone took care of you or helped you, they were showing compassion. Think of how good it felt to know that someone was helping you. Now you understand why compassion is so important.

- Think of someone you know who has compassion. Who are they? What kind of things do they do?

- Who is someone that is hard for you to show compassion to?

Part Three:

"COMPASSION"
IN THE BIBLE

I John 3:18 *Dear children, let us not love with words or tongue but with actions and in truth.*

If someone says to you, "You are my best friend," and then stomps on your foot and pulls your hair, you would probably wonder if they really are your friend. Why? Because their words said one thing, but their actions showed you something else. Their actions showed you the truth.

Our Bible verse says we should show each other that we love each other, not just say it. We need to show compassion to each other, not just say we have it.

In other words, if you see someone who fell and got hurt you should not just say, "Oh, that's too bad. I feel very bad for you." You should help them up.

Showing compassion means taking action! If you see someone with a need, don't just talk about it . . . do something!

• What is the difference between saying something and doing something?

• Why do actions show compassion better than words?

ACTION ACTIVITY: COMPASSION

Think of someone who is in a difficult situation, is hurt or ill, or needs cheering up. Try to come up with something you can do for them in secret. Maybe get some money together for a gift card from a favorite store, or make a gift for them, or create an awesome card for them. Try to get it to them secretly, so they don't know who made it or gave it.

• How did it feel to do something nice for someone in secret, knowing they would not find out who did it and never thank you for it?

"COMPASSION" IN THE STORY

The man who could not walk in the story lived in a time when the only way he could survive was if he had help. He could not work, so he had to beg for food or money. But because he could not walk, he could not get to the places where there were people with food and money. His four friends were probably the people who took him to the places where he could beg in the day and then would take him to whatever he called his home at night.

These were good friends. They were dedicated friends. And they helped him because they had compassion. They saw he had a need, so they helped him.

And they brought him to Jesus. They had heard of someone who could give their friend more help, so they wanted to get him there. They weren't going to let anything stand in their way. Not a crowd of people, anyway. If they couldn't go through the crowd, they were going to go over the crowd!

They went into action . . . and cut a hole in a roof!

And their work paid off. When everything was all over, their compassion resulted in their friend being able to walk!

• How do you think the man who could not walk felt when his friends helped him like they did?

• How did the friends show the kind of compassion that comes from our Bible verse: "with action and truth"?

Part Five

"COMPASSION" IN OUR LIVES

Do you have a friend who needs you to cut a hole in somebody's roof so you can lower him or her down through it? Probably not.

But do you know someone who needs help? Do you know someone going through a tough time? Do you know someone who is hurt or sick? Do you know someone who is sad or lonely? You probably do.

Those are people who need your compassion. Sometimes it is easy to know what to do. Someone who falls down might just need some help getting up. Someone who has their hands full might just need help opening a door. Someone who got their feelings hurt might just need a soft pat on the back or to be cheered up by a silly joke.

But sometimes you need to find creative ways to show compassion. If you have a friend who is having family troubles, you might have to take some time to figure out what you can do for them. Maybe they need someone they can talk to who will listen, or maybe they need someone who they can just play a game of catch with so they don't have to think about their problems.

Compassion can mean work. Hard work, sometimes. And sometimes it can take time. Sometimes you have to think hard about it and be creative. But when you show compassion to someone, it is rewarding to see someone who was feeling bad or sad start to feel better.

• Think of someone who is going through a tough time. How can you be like the friends of the man who couldn't walk and help that person?

• What are some hard times to show compassion?

THE BIG CATCH

Hero: Simon Peter
Hero Trait: Obedience
Key Verse: John 15:14
Story From: Luke 5:1-11

WITH THE CROWDS FOLLOWING HIM, JESUS FOUND IT HARDER TO FIND PLACES TO TEACH THEM.

HE CAME ACROSS SOME MEN HE HAD MET BEFORE, WHO WERE JUST COMING IN FROM FISHING.

HELLO, FRIENDS!

COULD I BORROW YOUR BOAT FOR A WHILE?

WHY NOT?

IT'S NOT DOING US ANY GOOD!

WE CAUGHT NOTHING LAST NIGHT!

I JUST NEED A PLACE TO BE ABLE TO TEACH THE PEOPLE.

PLEASE, JUST GO OUT A LITTLE BIT FROM THE SHORE.

WE CAN DO THAT.

THANK YOU.

AND JESUS TAUGHT THE PEOPLE. WHEN HE WAS FINISHED...

THANK YOU AGAIN, PETER. I AM SORRY TO HEAR OF YOUR POOR CATCH LAST NIGHT.

IT HAPPENS.

WE'LL TRY AGAIN TONIGHT.

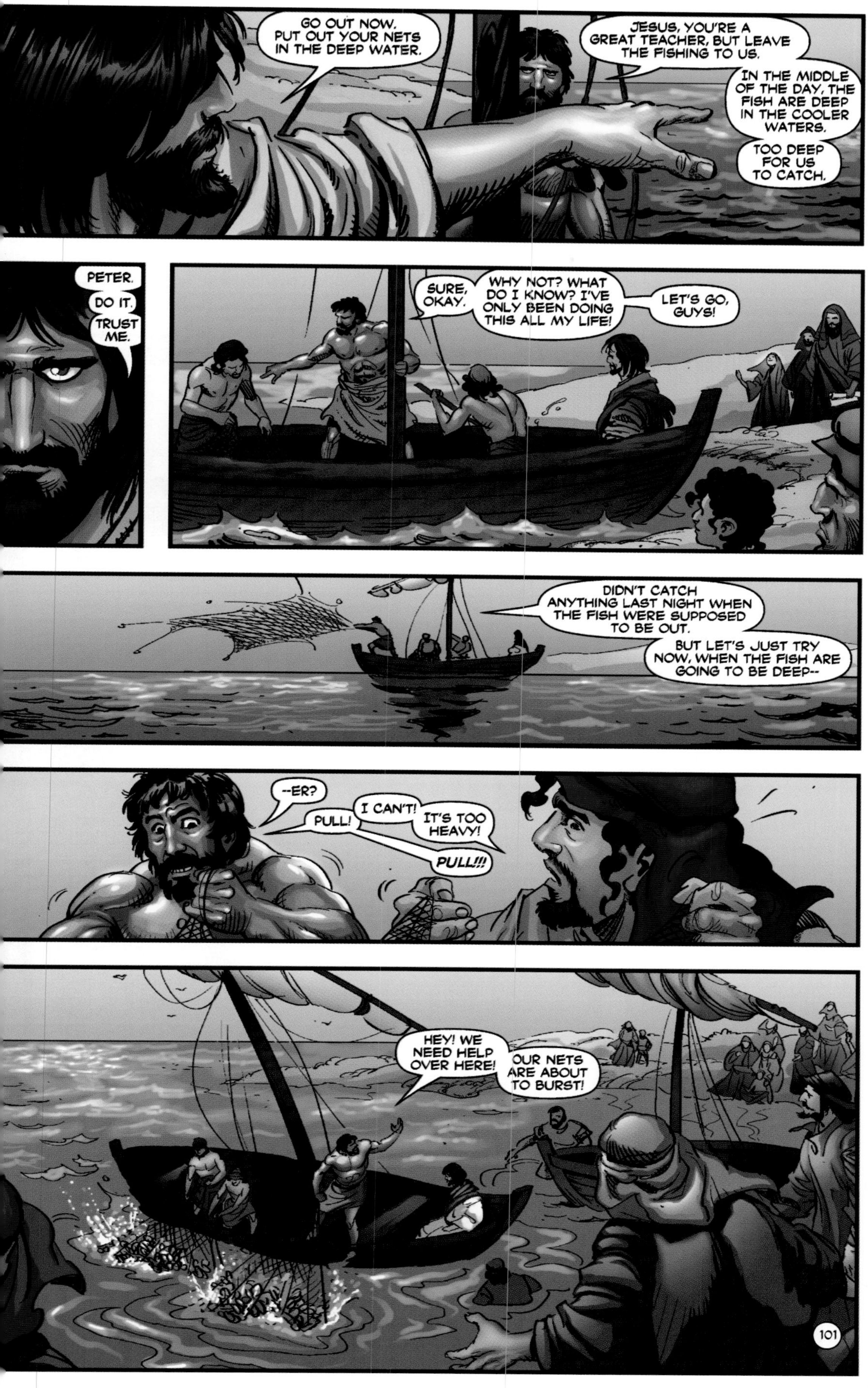
GO OUT NOW, PUT OUT YOUR NETS IN THE DEEP WATER.
JESUS, YOU'RE A GREAT TEACHER, BUT LEAVE THE FISHING TO US.
IN THE MIDDLE OF THE DAY, THE FISH ARE DEEP IN THE COOLER WATERS.
TOO DEEP FOR US TO CATCH.
PETER.
DO IT.
TRUST ME.
SURE, OKAY.
WHY NOT? WHAT DO I KNOW? I'VE ONLY BEEN DOING THIS ALL MY LIFE!
LET'S GO, GUYS!
DIDN'T CATCH ANYTHING LAST NIGHT WHEN THE FISH WERE SUPPOSED TO BE OUT.
BUT LET'S JUST TRY NOW, WHEN THE FISH ARE GOING TO BE DEEP--
--ER?
PULL!
I CAN'T!
IT'S TOO HEAVY!
PULL!!!
HEY! WE NEED HELP OVER HERE!
OUR NETS ARE ABOUT TO BURST!

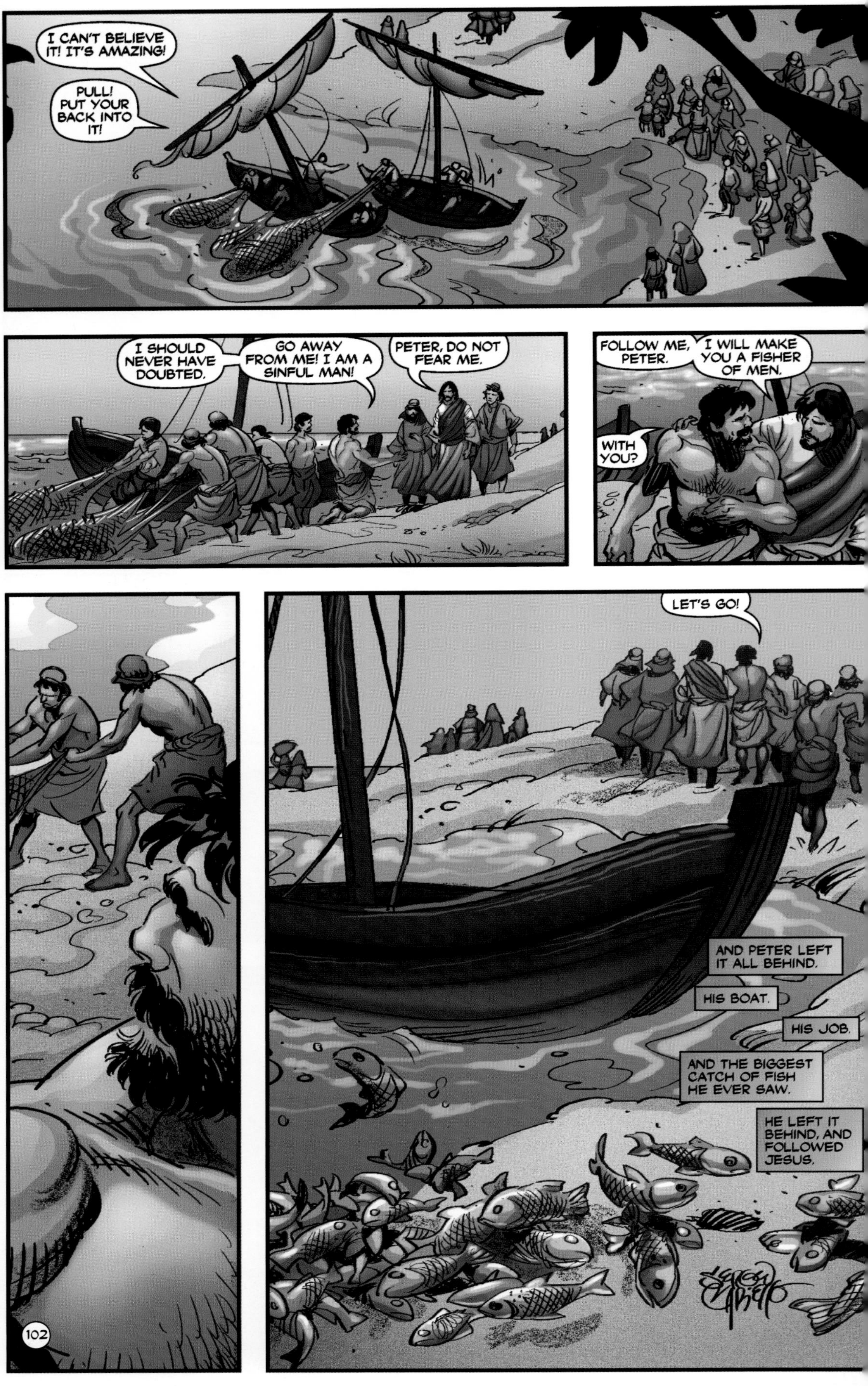
I CAN'T BELIEVE IT! IT'S AMAZING!
PULL! PUT YOUR BACK INTO IT!
I SHOULD NEVER HAVE DOUBTED.
GO AWAY FROM ME! I AM A SINFUL MAN!
PETER, DO NOT FEAR ME.
FOLLOW ME, PETER.
I WILL MAKE YOU A FISHER OF MEN.
WITH YOU?
LET'S GO!
AND PETER LEFT IT ALL BEHIND.
HIS BOAT.
HIS JOB.
AND THE BIGGEST CATCH OF FISH HE EVER SAW.
HE LEFT IT BEHIND, AND FOLLOWED JESUS.

Part Two:
"OBEDIENCE"

OBEDIENCE: *Doing what someone in authority has asked you to do.*

As children, one of the first things we learn is to obey our parents. Obedience is probably something that you have been learning since you first started to crawl!

Obedience is doing what someone in authority has asked you to do. It does not mean that you just do anything and everything any adult tells you to do. But God has put people in your life who are in authority, like your parents, your teachers, police, and other people.

Everywhere you go there are things that have to be obeyed, like rules in a classroom. Your teacher needs rules in the classroom so it is a safe and positive place for learning. Or traffic signs. Imagine what would happen if people never obeyed stop signs or traffic lights or speed limits!

And most importantly, we are to obey God. We are not only to obey the rules he has given us, but we are to listen to him for guidance and instruction. This is when you use wisdom and attentiveness together. You need attentiveness so you can know what God is asking you. You need wisdom so you can make sure what you do is obedient to God.

- Not including your parents, who are some people or what are some things that you have to obey?

- What would happen if people did not obey the many rules we have?

Part Three:
"OBEDIENCE" IN THE BIBLE

John 15:14 *You are my friends if you do what I command.*

Jesus said this. When he said this, he was not saying that he only likes you if you obey him.

No, he is saying something else. Something that you have read about earlier in this book. He is saying that if you love him, you will not just say it, you will show it. Your actions show that you are his friend. And what kind of action shows that you love him? Obeying the commands he has given us.

It is easy to find many of God's commands. But sometimes it is not as easy to follow them. If you did something you shouldn't have done and one of your parents asks you if you did it, it is easy to know what to do. You know you should tell the truth. That is one of God's commands. But, as they say, it is "easier said than done." Telling the truth means you have to take responsibility for your actions in this situation and that might mean consequences you don't want.

Obedience is not always easy. Obeying God's commands is sometimes very hard. But obeying God is always right, and always best. And obeying God is the best way to show that you love him.

- Where can you find God's commands?

- How does following God's commands show love to him?

Peter obeyed Jesus in two different ways in this story.

First, he listened to Jesus when Jesus told him to go back out and try again to catch fish, even though Peter had already tried.

In this situation, Jesus told Peter to do something different so Peter could get two blessings. The first blessing was lots of fish! The second blessing was that Peter could see Jesus' power. Imagine being there and seeing this happen!

But Peter also obeyed Jesus in a much more important way. Jesus told Peter, "Follow me." And Peter, after seeing what Jesus did, followed!

"Follow me," is Jesus' first command to us. He wants us all to follow him. Following Jesus is obeying him. It is doing the things he taught us about. It is following God's commands from the Bible. It is having the character traits found in this book . . . and so much more!

And as Peter learned, following Jesus is very rewarding. The fish he got was not the reward. Remember, he left that behind! The reward was seeing Jesus help people and learning from Jesus, and then taking what he learned and showing it to other people.

Obeying God is hard sometimes, but it is also well worth it.

- Why might Peter have chosen not to obey Jesus about the fishing nets?
- Why did Peter do as Jesus asked him to do?

Part Five:
"OBEDIENCE" IN OUR LIVES

One thing to remember is that even though obeying God is not always easy, God is always with us and he will help us.

Another thing to remember is that even when we mess up and don't do something we should have (like if we did lie in the earlier situation), we can talk to God about it. We can apologize and God forgives us. Hopefully, we are teachable and learn from that lesson.

Part of obeying God is obeying our parents. Part of obeying God is obeying other people who have been put in authority over us. But remember, we must use wisdom when we are obeying people, because sometimes people may ask us to do things that God would not want us to do. And God's rules always come before rules made by people.

If we obey God's commands, we show that we love him. And one of God's commands is that we love one another. Obeying God will help other people know about him, because you are showing his love to them. Obeying God helps your relationships with your friends, your family, your enemies, and, most importantly, with God himself!

- What are some ways to make obeying God easier?
- How does obeying God make your relationships with other people better?

ACTION ACTIVITY: OBEDIENCE

Get a blindfold and covers someone's eyes with it. Put them on one side of the room and while they are blindfolded, move the furniture to make obstacles for them to cross the room. Now, still blindfolded, have someone who can see the room give instructions, telling them what to do to get around the new layout of the room. (Give everyone a chance to do it.)

- How did it feel getting instructions while you were blindfolded? Did it make a difference knowing that the other person could see?
- How is this like following Jesus?

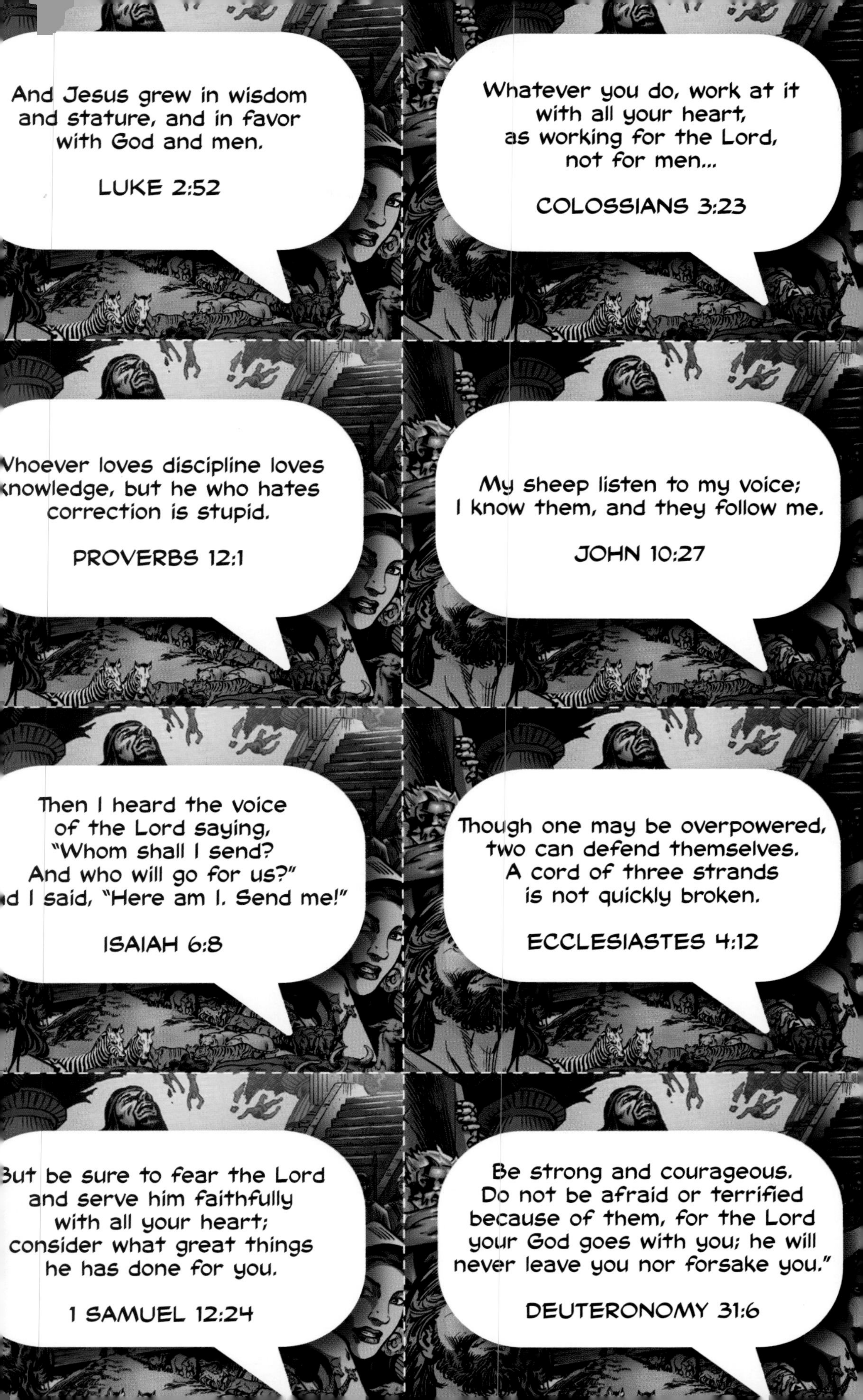

And Jesus grew in wisdom and stature, and in favor with God and men.
LUKE 2:52
Whatever you do, work at it with all your heart, as working for the Lord, not for men...
COLOSSIANS 3:23
Vhoever loves discipline loves knowledge, but he who hates correction is stupid.
PROVERBS 12:1
My sheep listen to my voice; I know them, and they follow me.
JOHN 10:27
Then I heard the voice of the Lord saying, "Whom shall I send? And who will go for us?" d I said, "Here am I. Send me!"
ISAIAH 6:8
Though one may be overpowered, two can defend themselves. A cord of three strands is not quickly broken.
ECCLESIASTES 4:12
But be sure to fear the Lord and serve him faithfully with all your heart; consider what great things he has done for you.
1 SAMUEL 12:24
Be strong and courageous. Do not be afraid or terrified because of them, for the Lord your God goes with you; he will never leave you nor forsake you."
DEUTERONOMY 31:6

The Big Boat
Hero: Noah
Hero Trait: Diligence

COLOSSIANS 3:23

Growing Up
Hero: Jesus
Hero Trait: Growth

LUKE 2:52

**Earth, Wind, Fire,
and Whispers**
Hero: Elijah
Hero Trait: Attentiveness

JOHN 10:27

**The Stinkiest
Time-Out Ever**
Hero: Jonah
Hero Trait: Teachability

PROVERBS 12:1

The Vegetable Test
Hero: Shadrach,
Meshach, & Abednego
Hero Trait: Friendship

ECCLESIASTES 4:12

**The Girl Who Didn't
Want to Be Queen**
Hero: Esther
Hero Trait: Availability

ISAIAH 6:8

The Furnace
Hero: Shadrach,
Meshach, & Abednego
Hero Trait: Courage

DEUTERONOMY 31:6

The Idol
Hero: Shadrach,
Meshach, & Abednego
Hero Trait: Faithfulness

1 SAMUEL 12:24

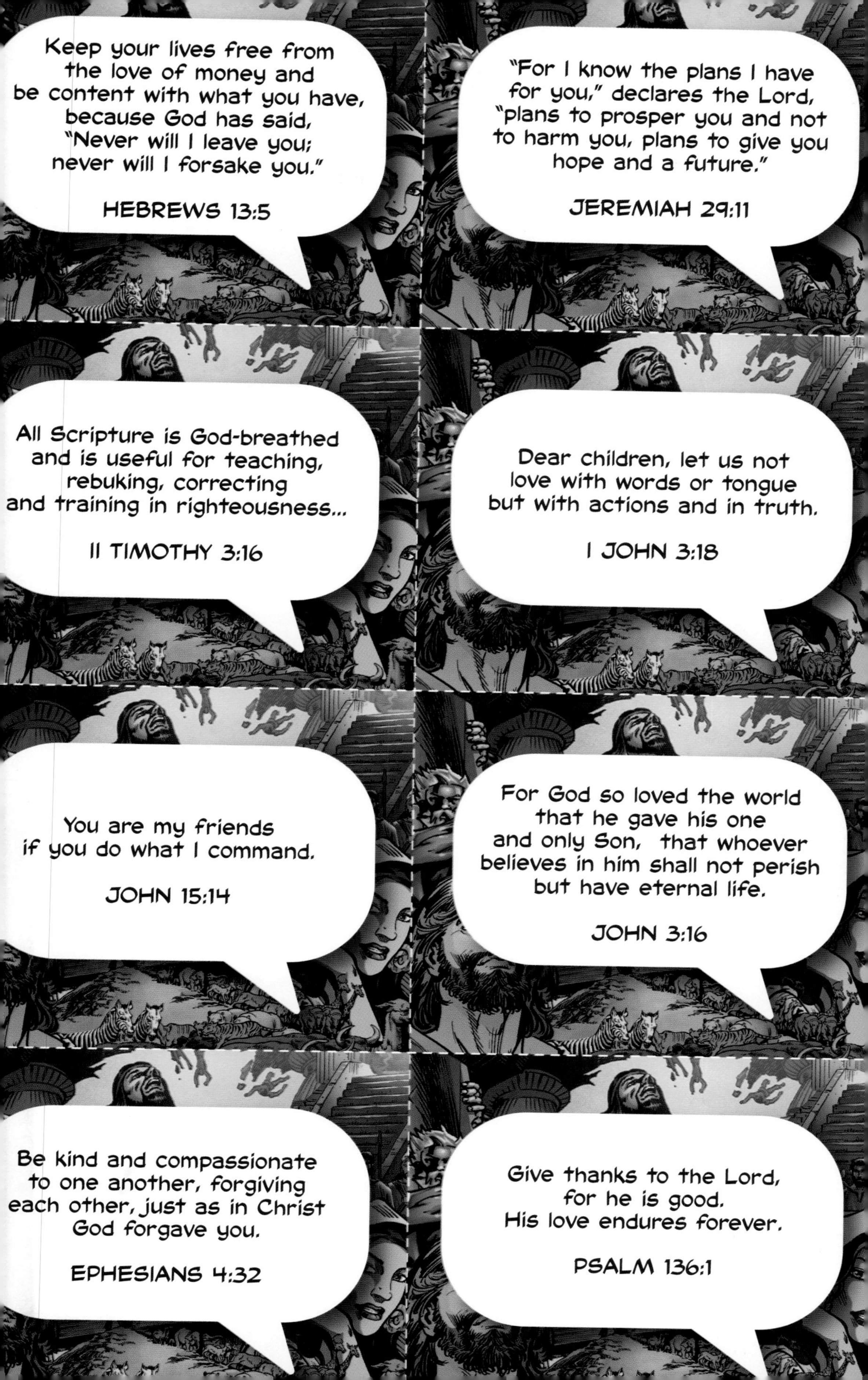
Keep your lives free from the love of money and be content with what you have, because God has said, "Never will I leave you; never will I forsake you."
HEBREWS 13:5
"For I know the plans I have for you," declares the Lord, "plans to prosper you and not to harm you, plans to give you hope and a future."
JEREMIAH 29:11
All Scripture is God-breathed and is useful for teaching, rebuking, correcting and training in righteousness...
II TIMOTHY 3:16
Dear children, let us not love with words or tongue but with actions and in truth.
I JOHN 3:18
You are my friends if you do what I command.
JOHN 15:14
For God so loved the world that he gave his one and only Son, that whoever believes in him shall not perish but have eternal life.
JOHN 3:16
Be kind and compassionate to one another, forgiving each other, just as in Christ God forgave you.
EPHESIANS 4:32
Give thanks to the Lord, for he is good. His love endures forever.
PSALM 136:1

The Long Wait
Hero: Anna the Prophetess
Hero Trait: Perseverence

JEREMIAH 29:11

The Baby and the Barn
Hero: Mary & Joseph
Hero Trait: Contentment

HEBREWS 13:5

Through the Roof
Hero: The Four Friends
Hero Trait: Compassion

I JOHN 3:18

The Big Battle
Hero: Jesus
Hero Trait: Wisdom

II TIMOTHY 3:16

For God so loved the world
that he gave his one and only Son,
that whoever believes in him
shall not perish but have eternal life.

JOHN 3:16

The Big Catch
Hero: Simon Peter
Hero Trait: Obedience

JOHN 15:14

Give thanks to the Lord,
for he is good.
His love endures forever.

PSALM 136:1

Be kind and compassionate
to one another, forgiving each oth
just as in Christ God forgave you

EPHESIANS 4:32

Also available from Kingstone Media

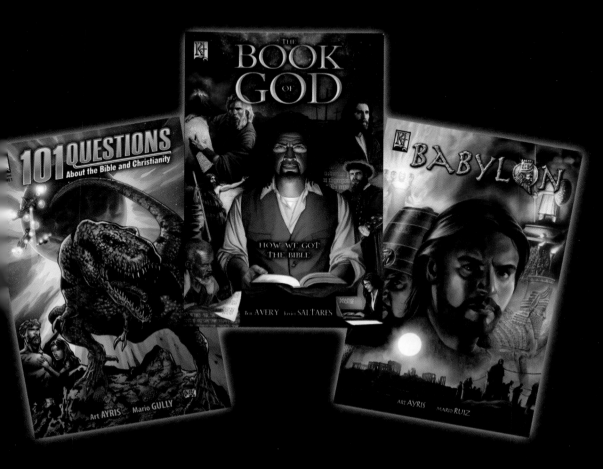

KingstoneComics.com

KINGSTONE
COMICS

Also available from Kingstone Media

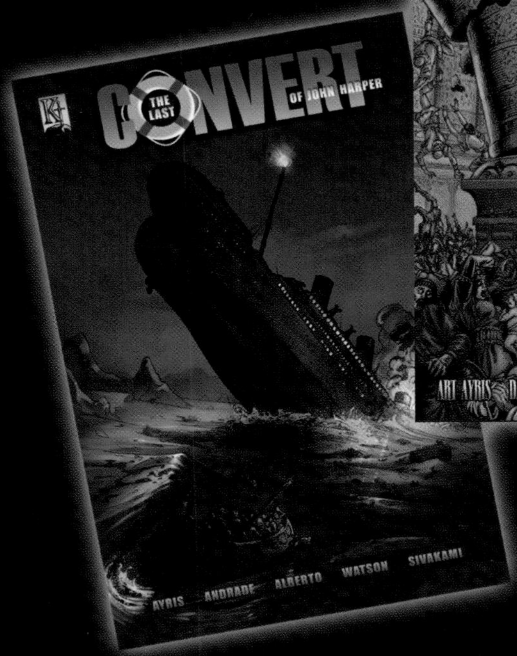
THE LAST CONVERT OF JOHN HARPER
AYRIS ANDRADE ALBERTO WATSON SIVAKAMI

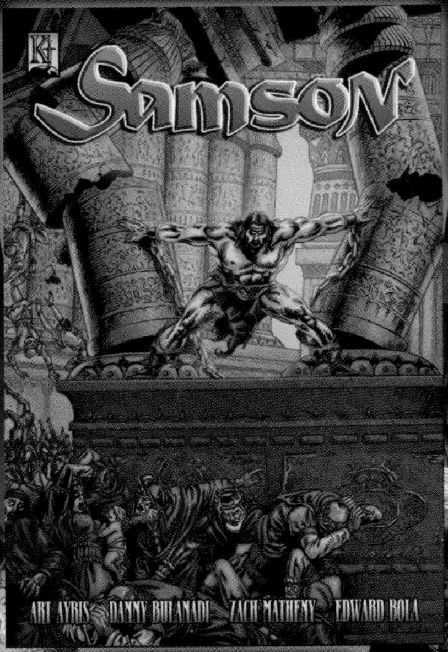
Samson
ART AYRIS DANNY BULANADI ZACH MATHENY EDWARD BOLA

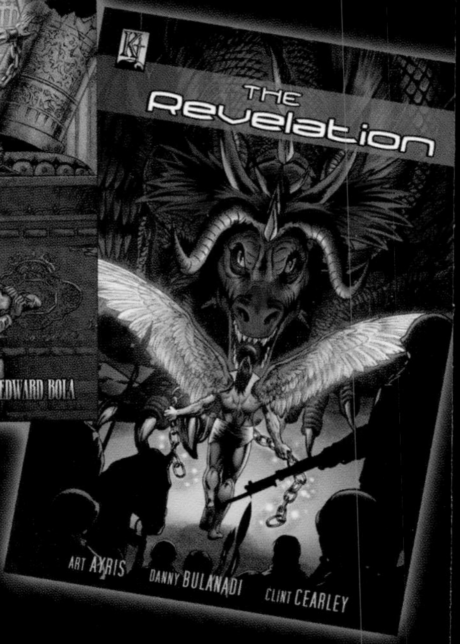
THE Revelation
ART AYRIS DANNY BULANADI CLINT CEARLEY

KingstoneComics.com

KINGSTONE
COMICS